# Seven Wonders of the World and More

by

DON BLATTNER

COPYRIGHT © 1998 Mark Twain Media, Inc.

ISBN 1-58037-073-X

Printing No. CD-1873

Mark Twain Media, Inc., Publishers
Distributed by Carson-Dellosa Publishing Company, Inc.

# Table of Contents

# Introduction

Throughout history humans have marveled at their accomplishments. Over the years, many people have listed these accomplishments and labeled them: *Wonders of the World*. Most of the lists have long since been forgotten, but one has survived, and the wonders listed are known today as *The Seven Wonders of the Ancient World*. The list was written by a Greek poet named Antipater, and it is not known why he put the list together. Was it just an opportunity to boast of the accomplishments of the human race? Maybe he wrote the list to preserve history for generations yet unborn. Or it might have been compiled merely as a guide for sailors, adventurers, or travelers. In any case, his list is a record of some of the most amazing structures in ancient times, and if he had not written about them, some may not be remembered today. Here are the seven wonders Antipater compiled.

1. The Great Pyramid of Giza
2. The Hanging Gardens of Babylon
3. The Statue of Zeus at Olympia
4. The Temple of Artemis at Ephesus
5. The Mausoleum at Halicarnassus
6. The Colossus of Rhodes
7. The Lighthouse of Alexandria

How did Antipater choose what to include on his list? It is apparent there are certain characteristics that each structure on the list has in common. All were created by humans and all are remarkable because of their size, beauty, or the engineering techniques used to create them. Also, all on the list were located around the Mediterranean. Obviously, Antipater only included wonders that were located near Greece, since these are the only ones he could possibly know about. There were, of course, wonders that existed in other parts of the world that many would argue were more magnificent than some of those on the list.

These Seven Wonders of the Ancient World were built over a time period that lasted more than half of recorded history and included structures from Egypt, Babylon, and Greece. Eventually, of the original Seven Wonders of the Ancient World, all but the pyramids were destroyed. In spite of the fact that most from the original list no longer exist, their descriptions still excite wonder and awe in those who read about them.

The first part of this book takes a brief look at the Seven Wonders of the Ancient World compiled by Antipater over 2,000 years ago. Then each of these wonders are explained and examined in detail. Related information pertaining to the structure and to the people who created it is included.

The second part of the book deals with other Wonders of the World that might easily have been included in a list of greatest human achievements. Some of these wonders existed at about the same time as the original Seven Wonders and some are more modern human achievements. Some time is also devoted to Natural Wonders of the World.

Name _____ Date _____

# The Seven Wonders of the Ancient World

About 120 B.C., a Greek poet named Antipater compiled a list that has become known as *The Seven Wonders of the Ancient World.* These wonders were the most remarkable structures created by human beings between the years of about 3000 B.C. to A.D. 280. They are called wonders because of their immense size, beauty, or architectural innovation. Since the list was made by a Greek at a time when travel to distant countries was rare, it is not surprising that all of the wonders were found in the region close to Greece. Had Antipater known about the Great Wall of China, which was begun in the third century B.C. and took hundreds of years to complete, or Stonehenge, which was built at about the same time as the pyramids, he might have included them. Here are the seven wonders Antipater compiled.

1. The Great Pyramid of Giza
2. The Hanging Gardens of Babylon
3. The Statue of Zeus at Olympia
4. The Temple of Artemis at Ephesus
5. The Mausoleum at Halicarnassus
6. The Colossus of Rhodes
7. The Lighthouse of Alexandria

**The Great Pyramid at Giza.** The pyramids are the oldest of the ancient wonders and the only structures on the list still standing. The three pyramids were built as tombs for, and by, Egyptian kings in about 2580 B.C. The Egyptian kings were Khufu, Khafre, and Menkure. The largest pyramid, the Great Pyramid, is about 450 feet high and each side is 755 feet long at its base.

**The Hanging Gardens of Babylon.** Babylon was a rich and powerful ancient city along the Euphrates River where modern Baghdad, the capital of Iraq, is now located. Babylon had many beautiful buildings, and one of the most beautiful was the Hanging Gardens, which was a huge, terraced building planted with every kind of tree and flower available in the kingdom. The Gardens were built by Nebuchadnezzar II, who ruled Babylon from 605 to 562 B.C. He built the Hanging Gardens for Amytis, his wife, who was homesick for her native country, Persia, which had hills, trees, flowers, and plants.

**The Temple of Artemis at Ephesus.** In about 560 B.C., Croesus, the King of Lydia, had a glorious temple built in Ephesus, a Greek city on the coast of Asia Minor that is now part of present-day Turkey. The temple, built of limestone and marble, was dedicated to the Greek goddess Artemis. Artemis, a protector of animals and young girls, was considered their main goddess. The Romans called this goddess "Diana."

**The Statue of Zeus at Olympia.** Olympia in Greece, a religious center where priests lived, was the location for many religious festivals and activities. Today, people know of Olympia because it is the place where the Olympic Games began. In the fifth century B.C., however, it was famous as the location of the magnificent statue of Zeus, the king of the gods. The statue, covered in ivory, gold, and precious stones, was completed about 450 B.C. and was probably the most famous statue in the ancient world. The Greek sculptor, Phidias of Athens, was the creator of this majestic sculpture.

**The Mausoleum at Halicarnassus.** Halicarnassus was the capital of a Greek city in Caria. Caria was on the coast of Asia Minor in what is now Turkey. The ruler of Caria was a man named Mausolus who had succeeded his father as governor. Mausolus was powerful and ambitious. With

Name _____ Date _____

money looted from victories in battle, he built the capital city of Halicarnassus and a beautiful palace for himself and his queen. He also planned a magnificent tomb that was completed after his death in 353 B.C. The tomb was so magnificent, that even today large tombs are called **mausoleums**.

   **The Colossus of Rhodes.** The people who lived on Rhodes, an island in the Aegean Sea off the coast of present-day Turkey, felt that Helios, the Greek sun-god, had saved their island from invaders. In gratitude, the people of Rhodes decided to build a special, large statue to honor him. The people chose Chares, an architect, to design the 120-foot statue, which was placed somewhere overlooking the harbor. The statue was called *the Colossus* from the Greek word *kolossos,* meaning "a huge statue." We do not know what the statue looked like, but it is likely that the Statue of Liberty, located in New York Harbor, was inspired by the Colossus. The Colossus was completed in about 290 B.C.

   **The Lighthouse of Alexandria.** The last of the Seven Wonders of the Ancient World was the Lighthouse of Alexandria, sometimes called the Pharos of Alexandria because it was built on the island of Pharos, just outside the harbor of Alexandria, Egypt. The lighthouse was so well-known in its time that the word *pharos* came to mean "lighthouse" in many languages. Designed by the Greek architect Sostratos, the lighthouse was about 400 feet tall, and the top tower held a fire that guided boats into the harbor. The lighthouse was completed in about 280 B.C.

## List and Locate the Seven Wonders of the Ancient World

   In the form below, list the Seven Wonders of the Ancient World and fill in the information concerning each.

| | Wonder | Location | Date Completed | Builder or Designer | Purpose |
|---|---|---|---|---|---|
| 1. | | | | | |
| 2. | | | | | |
| 3. | | | | | |
| 4. | | | | | |
| 5. | | | | | |
| 6. | | | | | |
| 7. | | | | | |

Name _____ Date _____

# The Seven Wonders of the Ancient World
## WHAT DID THEY LOOK LIKE?

You have read about the Seven Wonders of the Ancient World. Do you know what they may have looked like? While we don't know exactly how they appeared, we do have descriptions of most that have been handed down over the years. Below is a list of names of the Seven Wonders. In the space before each name on the list, put the letter of the appropriate Wonder.

_____ 1. The Great Pyramid of Giza

_____ 2. The Hanging Gardens of Babylon

_____ 3. The Statue of Zeus at Olympia

_____ 4. The Temple of Artemis at Ephesus

_____ 5. The Mausoleum at Halicarnassus

_____ 6. The Colossus of Rhodes

_____ 7. The Lighthouse of Alexandria

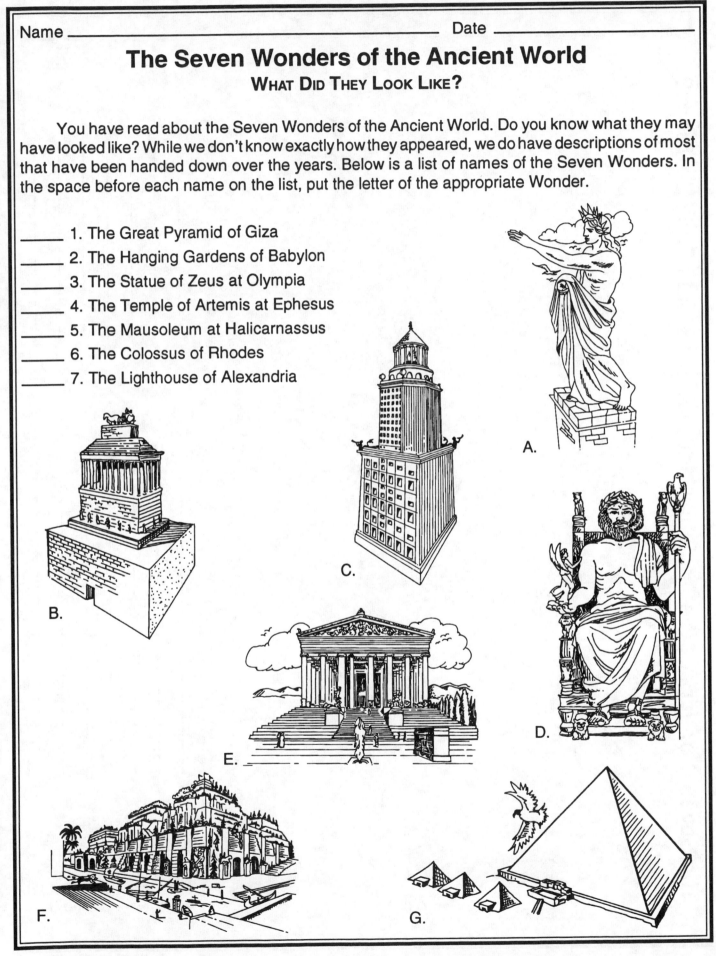

Name _____ Date _____

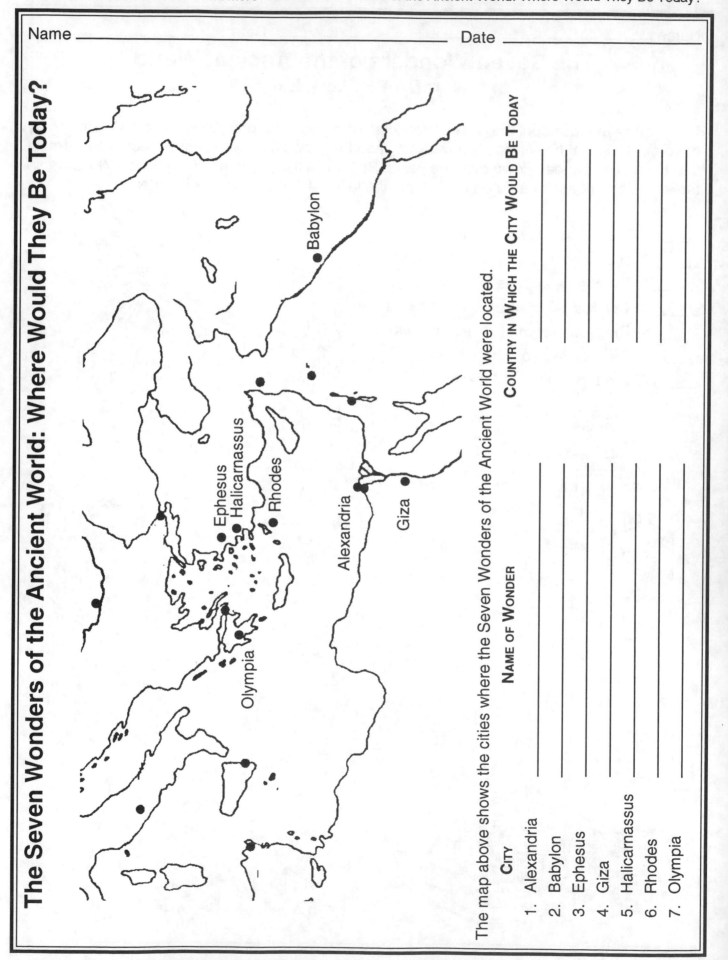

# The Seven Wonders of the Ancient World: Where Would They Be Today?

The map above shows the cities where the Seven Wonders of the Ancient World were located.

| CITY | NAME OF WONDER | COUNTRY IN WHICH THE CITY WOULD BE TODAY |
|---|---|---|
| 1. Alexandria | _____ | _____ |
| 2. Babylon | _____ | _____ |
| 3. Ephesus | _____ | _____ |
| 4. Giza | _____ | _____ |
| 5. Halicarnassus | _____ | _____ |
| 6. Rhodes | _____ | _____ |
| 7. Olympia | _____ | _____ |

# The Great Pyramid of Giza

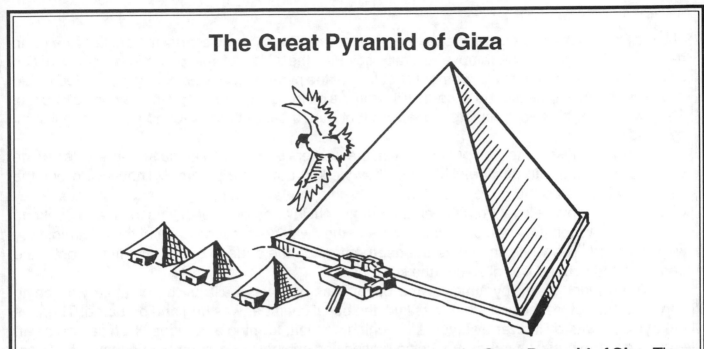

The oldest of the Seven Wonders of the Ancient World was the **Great Pyramid of Giza**. There were actually several pyramids built at Giza, which is located close to Cairo, Egypt's modern capital. The largest and the oldest of the pyramids was built as the tomb of **Khufu**, whom the Greeks called **Cheops**. Khufu was a **pharaoh**, which is what the king was called in ancient Egypt. It is only this large pyramid that is considered one of the original seven wonders, although two other pyramids built for Khufu's son and grandson and smaller pyramids built for their queens are located close by.

It may have taken over 20 years to build the Great Pyramid. While this seems like a long time, it should be remembered that most of the construction probably took place only three months of the year. Each year, the Nile River would flood between July and October. This annual event brought rich, fertile soil to the fields, but it prevented the farmers from working the land. It is likely that for these three months most men worked on the pyramid, hauling and placing stones. During the remaining nine months of the year, a smaller group of artisans and masons performed more intricate jobs and planned for the next construction season.

Another reason the construction took so long was that since construction took place about 5,000 years ago, there were no modern tools and machinery. Simple tools and manpower were used to build the pyramid. Over two and one-third million stone blocks, each weighing about two and one-half tons, were transported from a stone quarry on the other side of the Nile. Workers used bars to tip the huge stones to the side in order to slip a **sledge** underneath it. People in the United States use the term sled for sledge. The stone was tied to the sledge, raised, and set on top of round logs that had been placed parallel to each other on the ground. The workers were then able to pull the stone over the round logs, which made the stone easier to move. Once moved to the barge, the stone was taken across the Nile, unloaded, and the same method was used to transport the stone to the building site. The pyramid was built by stacking each level of stones on top of the last level, with each higher level being smaller than the level before. When the top level was completed, the sides looked like steps.

Throughout the centuries, people have wondered how the Egyptian workers were able to raise these very heavy stones up the side of the pyramid and place them on the upper levels. Many explanations have been offered, but the one commonly accepted today is that an earthen ramp was built on each side of the pyramid, making it possible to pull the stones up to the top. As each level of the pyramid was completed, the ramp was raised and lengthened so that the angle of the ramp remained the same. The ramp eventually covered the sides of the pyramid as construction advanced to the higher levels. Someone looking at the pyramid as it was nearly completed would have only seen a huge mound of earth with workers on top of the mound placing stones at the top. They would have been completely unaware that buried beneath the mound was a magnificent pyramid.

When the last stone was put into place, the workers began to fill in the step-like sides of the pyramid with white **limestone**. This time they worked down the pyramid. They would pull the limestone blocks up the ramp and fit the blocks into the levels forming a smooth surface. They would then remove a level from the earthen ramp, put in another level of limestone and continue the process. When they had completely worked their way down to the base of the pyramid, they were finished. The white limestone **encasement** made the surface of the pyramid smooth and beautiful and caused it to glisten in the sunlight.

The interior of the pyramid, or the burial chamber, was built as the pyramid was being constructed. Before the first stone was laid, the burial chamber was dug and prepared. Then, as the pyramid was built layer by layer, an opening was left, forming a corridor which served as an entrance to the burial chamber. For some reason, the original burial chamber beneath The Great Pyramid was not used, and a new burial chamber was built inside the pyramid itself.

The exact measurements of the Great Pyramid are difficult to determine. When the Great Pyramid was built, it was about 480 feet high, about as high as a 42-story skyscraper, but it is not that high today. The top levels of stones have been taken and used for other construction so that it is now about 30 feet less than its original height. In addition, the limestone casing, which gave the pyramid its gleaming surface, is also gone. These stones were also taken to be used in other buildings. Each side of its base measures about 756 feet, and, while each side is not identical, the difference between the longest and shortest side is less than 0.1 percent. This accuracy is surprising considering the primitive tools the Egyptians used.

## INSIDE THE PYRAMID

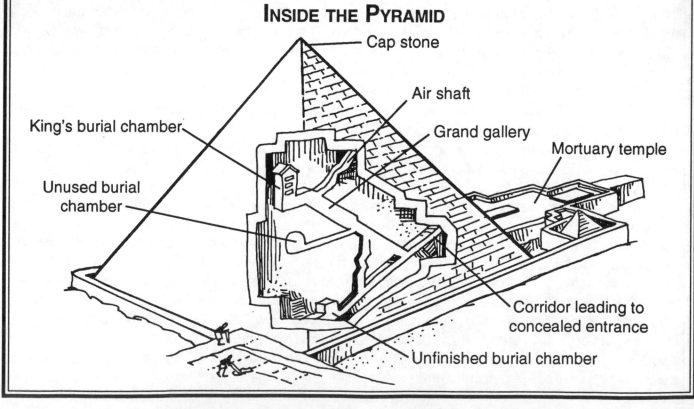

- Cap stone
- Air shaft
- King's burial chamber
- Grand gallery
- Mortuary temple
- Unused burial chamber
- Corridor leading to concealed entrance
- Unfinished burial chamber

Name _____ Date _____

# The Great Pyramid Quiz

Shown below are a number of sentences. Some are true and some are false. If the sentence is true, write the word "true" in front of the sentence. If the sentence is false, write a term that could replace the term written in bold type to make the sentence true.

_____ 1. Originally, the pyramid had an **alabaster** casing, which gave the pyramid its gleaming surface.

_____ 2. The accuracy of the construction is surprising, considering the **primitive** tools the Egyptians used.

_____ 3. A **pulley** was built on each side of the pyramid, making it possible to pull the stones up to the top.

_____ 4. There were **several** pyramids built at Giza.

_____ 5. In ancient Egypt the king was called **chief.**

_____ 6. Over two and one-third **billion** stones were used to build the Great Pyramid.

_____ 7. The Great Pyramid of Giza was built as a tomb for **King Tut.**

_____ 8. The pyramid is located close to **Alexandria**, Egypt's modern capital.

_____ 9. People in the United States use the term **sled** for sledge.

_____ 10. It may have taken over **20 years** to build the Great Pyramid.

_____ 11. Most of the construction on the pyramid probably took place only **nine** months of the year.

_____ 12. It is likely that most men worked on the pyramid when the **Mississippi** River was flooding the farm land.

_____ 13. Workers used bars to tip the huge stone to the side in order to slip a **wagon** underneath it.

_____ 14. The interior of the pyramid was the **astronomical observatory.**

_____ 15. Originally, the pyramid was 30 feet **lower** than it is today.

_____ 16. Each stone in the pyramid weighed over two and one-half **pounds** each.

_____ 17. The original height of the pyramid was about as high as a **42-story** skyscraper.

_____ 18. Each stone was tied to a sledge and set on top of **wheels**, making it easy to roll the stones to the building site.

_____ 19. The difference between the longest and shortest sides is within **10** percent.

_____ 20. For nine months of the year, artisans and masons performed the more **intricate** jobs.

# The Pyramids and Mummies

The function of the Great Pyramid, as well as all other ancient Egyptian pyramids and tombs, was to preserve the body after death. The need to preserve the body was not just custom, but an important part of the Egyptian religion. The ancient Egyptians believed that if a person's body was preserved on earth, the soul would have eternal life in the kingdom of **Osiris**, their god. Since bacteria causes a body to decay quickly after death, the Egyptians developed an embalming method known as **mummification** to preserve the body of the deceased. They also discovered that the hot, dry sand of the desert preserved the body better than the fertile earth close to the Nile. That is why the pyramids and burial grounds were placed in the desert away from the city and farmland.

It took 70 days to mummify a body. The deceased was placed on a table and the internal organs were removed to prevent decay. Then the body was bathed with wine and other liquids. The alcohol in the wine would kill decay-causing bacteria. Salt, called **natron**, was then packed around the body to dry it out. After 40 days, the skin became dry and leathery. The mummy was then cleaned again and rubbed with spices and oils to soften the skin.

While most Egyptians were buried naked in shallow graves, royalty and wealthy people were wrapped in linen with jewels and charms inserted in the layers of linen in order to protect the spirit of the deceased. The mummy was then given a face mask that resembled the deceased.

To protect the mummy from damage, it was placed in a coffin-like container called a **mummy case**. The style, shape and decoration of the mummy case evolved over the years. Originally, they were plain wooden boxes with simple decorations. They eventually took on the human shape and were extravagantly decorated. Pharaohs, royalty, and wealthy people were buried in a **sarcophagus**, which is a coffin made of stone. The sarcophagus, which was elaborately decorated and often in the shape of a body, served the same purpose as the mummy case. It protected the body.

Once the body was prepared, the funeral began. The mummy was put on a sled or was carried to the tomb. The funeral procession included servants who carried food and drink and the mummy's possessions, priests who chanted prayers from the **Book of the Dead**, family and friends of the deceased, and professional mourners. Professional mourners were women hired by the family to cry, wave their arms, and sob uncontrollably. Since a person's importance was judged by the number of mourners and their magnitude of grief, it was considered a sign of respect to hire as many mourners as possible.

When the mummy arrived at the tomb, a priest would perform a ritual called **"The Opening of the Mouth."** A priest would touch the mummy's mouth with a special instrument that was intended to enable the deceased to control his body again. The mummy was then placed in its tomb along with clay pots of food and water and other possessions that could be used in the afterlife. The mourners then had a feast at the door of the tomb in celebration that the deceased person's soul had arrived in the presence of Osiris to be judged.

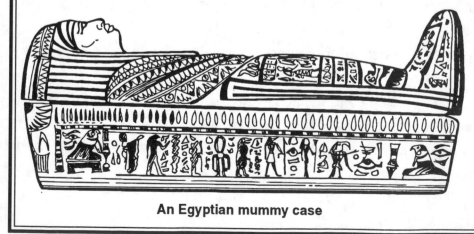

**An Egyptian mummy case**

# Strange Facts About Ancient Egyptian Burials

1. Ancient Egyptians thought that intelligence was in the heart, not the brain.
2. A bronze disc, which carried a spell, was placed under a mummy's head to keep it warm.
3. Mummies were buried facing east so they could see the sun rise each morning.
4. Eyes were sometimes painted on the side of the coffin so the mummy could see what was happening on the outside.
5. The chief embalmer wore a jackal mask representing *Anubis*, the god of mummification.
6. At the tomb, there would be a ceremony called "The Opening of the Mouth." The priest would touch the mummy's mouth with a special implement that was supposed to restore the mummy's senses so it could function in the afterlife.
7. The deceased might have several identical mummy cases, each larger than the next. The mummy would be placed in the smallest case, which would then be placed in the one slightly larger, which would then be placed in the next largest size, and so on.
8. Some tombs contained "Corn Mummies," which looked like real mummies, but inside the wrapped linen were grains of corn. The corn mummy had a mask of Osiris. The purpose of the corn mummy was to help the spirit of the deceased to join Osiris in the afterlife.
9. Ground-up mummies were used as medicine in the sixteenth century.
10. Ground-up mummies were also used to make a brown paint for artists.
11. In the sixteenth century, Egyptians would sometimes burn mummies as fuel.
12. Mummy heads were sold as souvenirs in the nineteenth century and displayed in homes.
13. Pets of the deceased were often mummified and placed in the tomb with their master.
14. Animals were identified with certain gods and were often mummified and buried in what we would call pet cemeteries. Mummies of bulls, baboons, birds, jackals, and even crocodiles have been found.
15. Cats were sacred, and anyone who killed a cat could be put to death. When a pet cat died, it was mummified, placed in a coffin, and buried.
16. When a pet cat died, a family might shave their eyebrows as a way to honor its pet.
17. In the nineteenth century, hundreds of thousands of cat mummies were shipped from Egypt to England, where they were turned into fertilizer.
18. Mummies can be examined without unwrapping them by using advanced electronic X-ray techniques. Scientists can determine the diseases the mummy had as well as a great deal of information about how he or she lived.
19. The Egyptians believed that you "can take it with you." They placed all sorts of personal belongings—games, beauty aids, and even food—in tombs to be enjoyed in the afterlife.
20. The sarcophagus of the last Egyptian pharaoh was taken to Alexandria, where the Greeks used it as a bathtub.

Name _____ Date _____

# Ancient Egyptian Terms

Listed below are a number of common words. In the blank to the right of each word, write the word or phrase associated with ancient Egypt that would be *similar* to the common word. Use the list of Egyptian terms given on the right side of the page.

**WORD LIST**

1. Ceremony _____  Amulet

2. Charm _____  Book of the Dead

3. Clerk _____  Bier

4. Coffin _____  Cartonnage

5. Embalmer _____  Catacombs

6. Embalming _____  Field of Reeds

7. God _____  Hieroglyphics

8. Heaven _____  Mummification

9. King _____  Mummy case

10. Mourners _____  Osiris

11. Paper _____  Overseer of Mysteries

12. Papier-mâché _____  Papyrus

13. Sled _____  Pharaoh

14. Stand _____  Pyramid

15. Tomb _____  Scribe

16. Tunnels _____  Sledge

17. Writing _____  Weepers

Name _____ Date _____

# Three World Conquerors Who Invaded Egypt

Alexander the Great, Julius Caesar, and Napoleon were all soldiers who led their troops into Egypt. How much do you know about each of these men? Listed below are statements that relate to one of the three conquerors. Before each statement are the letters "A," which represents Alexander, "C," which represents Caesar, and "N," which represents Napoleon. Circle the letter to whom the statement pertains.

A  C  N  1. He was born in Corsica.

A  C  N  2. His father was King Philip of Macedonia.

A  C  N  3. He became dictator of Rome.

A  C  N  4. He crowned himself Emperor of France.

A  C  N  5. His wife's name was Josephine.

A  C  N  6. He helped his father unite the Greek city-states into a single nation.

A  C  N  7. He said, "I came, I saw, I conquered."

A  C  N  8. One of his teachers was Aristotle.

A  C  N  9. He was involved in the civil war between Cleopatra and her brother.

A  C  N  10. He died on the island of St. Helena.

A  C  N  11. He allowed a statue of him to be carved and placed next to seven early kings of Rome.

A  C  N  12. Scholars accompanied him on his invasion of Egypt, studied the country, and eventually produced a detailed 24-volume history of Egypt.

A  C  N  13. Mark Antony was his military companion and friend.

A  C  N  14. He built a city by the Mediterranean where the Nile entered the sea. Then he named the city after himself.

A  C  N  15. He wrote the *Commentaries on the Gallic War*.

A  C  N  16. One of his men discovered *The Rosetta Stone*, which enabled scholars to read and understand hieroglyphics, the picture writing of ancient Egypt.

A  C  N  17. He invaded Egypt in 1798.

A  C  N  18. When he invaded Egypt, it was controlled by the Mameluk turks and was part of the Ottoman Empire.

A  C  N  19. When he invaded Egypt, it was controlled by Persians and was part of the Persian Empire.

A  C  N  20. The Egyptians treated him as a god and crowned him pharaoh of Egypt.

A  C  N  21. He made sacrifices to the Egyptian gods and ordered his men to rebuild temples other invaders had destroyed.

A  C  N  22. Legend says that one day he entered a pyramid alone and had a "mystical experience," which he refused to discuss with anyone.

A  C  N  23. He was stabbed and killed by Marcus Junius Brutus and others on March 15, the Ides of March, 44 B.C.

Name _____ Date _____

# Napoleon and the Pyramids

Napoleon Bonaparte invaded Egypt in 1798 and occupied Alexandria and Cairo. He was very interested in Egypt and their ancient customs and brought many scientists and scholars to excavate and study this early culture. The French scholars took many mummies, mummy cases, and other artifacts from the tombs and shipped them to France, where many are still on display in museums. Eventually, Napoleon helped create the *Institute of Egypt*, a scholarly organization to study ancient Egypt.

One day, as the French scholars were examining some of the items from a tomb, Napoleon went into a pyramid alone. He was there for a long time, and when he came out, he looked very solemn and thoughtful. Someone asked him what was wrong. They asked what he saw in the pyramid. Napoleon sharply replied that he had nothing to say and he never wanted to talk about it again. Near the end of his life, he almost told someone what he had seen, but then decided not to. He said, "You'd never believe me."

What did Napoleon see? A spirit of a dead pharaoh? A view of the afterlife? A vision showing his eventual defeat and exile? You decide. Suppose you are Napoleon. You have just come out of the tomb, and you decide to write to your wife, Josephine, and tell her what you have seen. Complete the letter below.

My Dearest Josephine,

_____

_____

_____

_____

_____

_____

_____

_____

_____

_____

_____

_____

_____

_____

# The Hanging Gardens of Babylon

Rising out of the arid, hostile desert in the seventh century B.C. was **Babylon**, one of the most beautiful and powerful cities in the world. The city was so magnificent it was called the "Gate of the Gods." The book of Revelations in the Holy Bible describes Babylon as the city "that was clothed in fine linen, and purple, and scarlet, and decked with gold, and precious stones, and pearls!" Such a description was well deserved. There were grandiose palaces and temples ascending into the heavens. The temples were tall, shaped like pyramids, and built using techniques that had never been used before. One huge temple rose three hundred feet above the ground and is referred to in the Bible as **"the Tower of Babel."**

Even the private homes in Babylon were superior to the homes of others in the region. While the exteriors of Babylonian homes were unimpressive, the interiors were spacious and comfortable. They were often two stories high with the bedrooms on the second story. In warm weather, however, the family often slept on the roof in order to catch a breeze. The first floor of a Babylonian home included a living room, dining room, kitchen, and chapel. The floors were made of baked brick. All of the rooms had beautiful and comfortable furniture. A unique feature of the Babylonian home was the interior court, which opened to the sky and provided air, light, and privacy.

Babylon had two other features that enhanced its wonder and beauty. One feature was an ornately decorated wall that surrounded the city. The wall was wide enough at the top to accommodate a four-horse chariot. There were also towers for guards who were stationed to watch for invaders and to offer protection during an attack. The wall had several gates so travelers could enter and leave the city, but the most famous gate was called **the Gate of Ishtar**.

Named for a goddess, the Gate of Ishtar was not only practical, it was beautiful. Glazed, enamel bricks were decorated with pictures of animals. So impressive was the gate and wall surrounding Babylon, it was originally included as one of the Seven Wonders of the Ancient World. The walls of Babylon were eliminated from the list of the Seven Wonders of the Ancient World and replaced by the Lighthouse of Alexandria. Why the change was made is unknown.

The second feature that enhanced the wonder and beauty of Babylon was built by Nebuchadnezzar. It is called **the Hanging Gardens of Babylon** and is still listed as one of the Seven Wonders of the Ancient World. Nebuchadnezzar reigned in Babylon from 605 B.C. to 562 B.C. and is credited with building much of Babylon. He not only built the magnificent wall and the

Ishtar Gate that protected the city, but he also built beautiful temples and palaces. His most famous structure, however, was the Hanging Gardens.

It is believed that Nebuchadnezzar had the Hanging Gardens built to please his wife **Amytis**, who was from a region in **Persia** that was cool and had an abundance of trees, plants, and flowers. Amytis did not like the desert and dreamed about the beautiful country she had left, so Nebuchadnezzar decided to build a rooftop garden—an artificial mountain—to remind her of her homeland.

The Hanging Gardens were constructed of brick and were actually a series of terraces, one above the other. Each terrace had soil and the gardens were planted with every kind of tree, plant, and flower available in the kingdom. In addition to the plants, it is believed that there were also pools and fountains.

While designing and building a structure strong enough to withstand the terrific weight of the trees and earth to grow them was difficult enough, determining how these plants could survive and prosper in the desert was even more of a challenge. Plants need water to survive, but Babylon rarely received any rain. This problem was solved by raising water from the **Euphrates River**. The exact manner in which water was raised to water the plants and trees on the terraces is unclear, but it is thought that the engineers devised an original watering system, which writers later called **"water engines."** Slaves probably lifted the water to the upper levels with the use of some sort of simple belt or treadmill, and once it had been raised, there may have been pipes, channels, or conduits to distribute the water to the plants.

The existence of the Hanging Gardens has been questioned because they were not described by writers who lived at the time when the Gardens were supposed to have been built. These writers wrote about events of the time and other buildings in the city, but not about the Hanging Gardens. Why? Certainly the Hanging Gardens deserved their attention, but they failed to describe them.

We only know about the gardens because of the writings of Greek and Roman authors, most of whom visited Babylon long after it was gone. These writers merely recorded stories about this magnificent structure told by the descendants of the Babylonians. One Roman writer, however, actually saw the Hanging Gardens many years after it had been neglected and had declined in beauty. He wrote a description of the structure, and archeologists have excavated ruins in the ancient city about 50 miles south of modern-day Baghdad in Iraq that are consistent with that description. This leads many to believe that the Hanging Gardens of Babylon did actually exist.

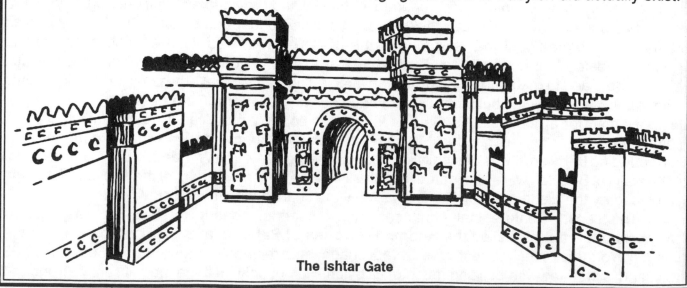

**The Ishtar Gate**

14

Name _____ Date _____

# The Hanging Gardens of Babylon Quiz

Shown below are a number of sentences. Some are true and some are false. If the sentence is true, write the word "true" in front of the sentence. If the sentence is false, write a term that could replace the term written in bold type to make the sentence true.

_____ 1. Private homes in Babylon were **inferior** to the homes of others in the region.

_____ 2. Homes in Babylon usually had a **chapel** for worship.

_____ 3. In warm weather, the family often slept **in the interior court**.

_____ 4. **Babylon** was one of the most beautiful and powerful cities in the world.

_____ 5. Babylon was so wonderful it was called the **"Garden of the Gods."**

_____ 6. Babylonian homes usually had **a family room**, which opened to the sky and provided air, light, and privacy.

_____ 7. The most famous gate into Babylon was called **The Gate of Ishtar**.

_____ 8. The Gate of Ishtar was not only practical, it was beautiful. Glazed, enamel bricks included pictures of **the goddess Ishtar**.

_____ 9. On the wall, guards were stationed to watch for **tourists**.

_____ 10. The wall surrounding the city was so thick that the top of the wall was wide enough to accommodate a **four-horse chariot**.

_____ 11. The gate and wall around the city were so grand, they were originally included as one of the **Seven Wonders of the Ancient World**.

_____ 12. The walls of Babylon were replaced on the list of the Seven Wonders of the Ancient World by the **Lighthouse of Alexandria**.

_____ 13. The Hanging Gardens of Babylon were built by **King Nebuchadnezzar**.

_____ 14. The King had the Hanging Gardens built to please his wife **Amytis**.

_____ 15. The King's wife was from a region in **Mesopotamia** that was cool and had an abundance of trees, plants, and flowers.

_____ 16. The garden was watered by raising water from the **Tigris** River.

_____ 17. Engineers devised an original watering system, which writers later called **"water engines."**

_____ 18. In addition to the plants, it is believed the gardens also had pools and **colorful birds**.

_____ 19. Writers of the time failed to mention the **Gate of Ishtar** in their writings.

_____ 20. Archaeologists have excavated ruins at a site described by a **Persian** writer that could be the Hanging Gardens.

# Create a Travel Brochure for the Hanging Gardens

Assume that King Nebuchadnezzar and the city of Babylon have fallen on tough times. They need money to run Babylon and to pay for all of the expensive temples that are being built. Nebuchadnezzar decides to finance these projects by opening up the Hanging Gardens to tourists. He wants everyone in the region to know they can visit this beautiful oasis in the middle of the desert. He hires you to create a brochure to be distributed throughout Mesopotamia and neighboring countries.

Use the form on the following page to create a brochure that tells people why they should visit the gardens. Fold the paper in thirds on the dashed lines and fill each panel with artwork, facts, and so on. Use your imagination. Include anything you think would encourage people to visit. Feel free to make up any features of the Garden that are not recorded. Ask yourself: "What will the visitors see?", "What would encourage them to come?", "How long will the tour last?", and "What will they do?".

Use the lines below to organize the information you intend to include before you begin making the actual brochure.

_____

_____

_____

_____

_____

_____

_____

_____

_____

_____

_____

_____

_____

_____

_____

_____

# Visit

## The World Famous

## Hanging Gardens

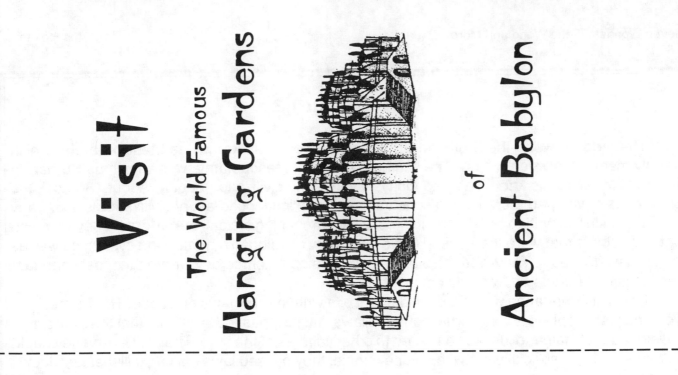

## of

## Ancient Babylon

# Mesopotamia

The land between the Tigris and Euphrates Rivers was known as **Mesopotamia**, which literally means "between rivers." The southern region of Mesopotamia was known as **Sumer**. In this location, which is known as Iraq today, a very early civilization began. About 1800 B.C. the Sumerians developed a civilization so advanced that it influenced every civilization since. They invented a kind of writing based on pictures, which archeologists call **cuneiform**. They wrote on wet clay tablets that were then baked in the sun. They developed a numbering system as well as vehicles with wheels. They were also the first to develop a democracy where the most important decisions were made by free adult men.

Of great importance was the development of a written list of laws or a code. The **Sumerians** were the first people to actually write down the laws that they passed. The laws that the Sumerians developed were fair and just as compared to other cultures of the time. They felt everyone should be treated fairly, especially the weak. For example, they passed laws making it illegal for widows and orphans to be taxed.

Having laws written down was important so a ruler or judge would not be able to change or interpret laws as they chose. This was especially important in Sumer, since the judges were not paid professionals as they are today. They had other jobs and were only part-time judges who did not get paid for their services. It would be tempting to receive money in order to decide a case a certain way. Written laws make it difficult for a dishonest judge to give special treatment to the rich or to ignore the concerns of the poor or weak.

Another way the Sumerians made sure officials acted honestly was with the use of clay to enclose important documents. Any time a Sumerian bought or sold something, was married, or went to court, the contract or information concerning the transaction was written on a clay tablet, and then the tablet was sealed in a **clay envelope**. The envelope was like a jar and no one was able to take the contract out of the envelope without breaking it. If there was a dispute about the contract, the parties involved took the envelope to a judge who broke it open, read the contract, and then made a ruling.

In Sumer any person could take a complaint to the court in order to have the complaint resolved. Both sides would tell their sides of the stories, the judges would also listen to the witnesses, and a **scribe** would write down everything that was said on a clay tablet, which was then sealed in an envelope. In many respects, a trial in Sumer almost 4,000 years ago was very similar to a trial today.

The laws in Sumer would be considered humane today. If you did something wrong or injured someone, there was usually a fine. However, the fine varied according to *who was injured*. For example, if a person injured someone of the same rank as he, then there would be a fine. If he injured a **freed man** in the same way (a freed man was a slave who had been freed), the fine would be less. If he injured a slave in the same way, the fine would be even less. So even though there was equality in the law for all citizens of Sumer, the fairness did not apply to everyone. Even so, the written laws developed by the Sumerians were very advanced and fair for the time. More importantly, they provided the framework for other codes or laws that followed. Most notable was Hammurabi's code, which was based on the Sumerian sense of justice.

Name _____    Date _____

# Hanging Gardens of Babylon Crossword Puzzle

Use the clues below to complete the crossword puzzle.

## ACROSS

1. A river running past Babylon
3. The people who lived in Sumer
5. The land between the Tigris and Euphrates Rivers
10. King of Babylon who had the Hanging Gardens built for his wife
12. Term that refers to the body that decides a case of law or the place where it is decided
14. The southern region of Mesopotamia
17. A book in the Holy Bible that describes Babylon
19. A room used for worship found in every Babylonian home
21. In addition to plants, the Hanging Gardens had pools and _____.
22. One who has been freed from slavery

## DOWN

2. The shape of Babylonian temples
4. The material used to make tablets for writing

6. A rich and powerful ancient civilization; it was located where Iran is located today
7. One of the two rivers that were located on either side of Mesopotamia
8. The modern country located in the area that was once called Mesopotamia.
9. The Hanging Gardens were a series of _____.
11. Sometimes used in place of the word *law*
12. A type of writing used by the Sumerians; the characters were wedge-shaped.
13. The Hanging Gardens got their water from water _____.
15. Sumerian contracts were sealed in a clay _____.
16. The goddess after whom the gate to Babylon was named
18. A huge temple referred to in the Bible
20. One of the most beautiful and powerful cities in the world in the seventh century B.C.

Name _____ Date _____

# Hammurabi's Code

Hammurabi was a king of Babylonia in southern Mesopotamia and probably ruled for about 40 years, beginning in 1792 B.C. Babylon was but one of several kingdoms in Mesopotamia, but when Hammurabi was king, he conquered the leaders of the other kingdoms and created an enlarged Mesopotamian state. Hammurabi was not only an excellent military leader, he was a skilled administrator as well. His crowning achievement was a code of laws he had drawn up. This code is known as *Hammurabi's Code*. These laws were taken, for the most part, from the written laws developed by the Sumerians and covered every aspect of Babylonian life. Hammurabi's Code, however, had an additional element—*revenge*. In Sumer the punishment for crimes was usually a fine. Hammurabi's Code added the ancient custom of "*an eye for an eye, and a tooth for a tooth.*" In other words, if you do something bad to a person, the court will retaliate and do the same thing to you. The Holy Bible makes similar references to punishment. In Exodus 21:12-27, the Bible says, "Life for life, eye for eye, tooth for tooth, hand for hand, foot for foot." Deuteronomy 19:21 says, "Whoever strikes a man a mortal blow must be put to death."

Like the Sumerians, however, a person's punishment depended on who was wronged. For example, if a man put out the eye of another man, his eye would be put out. But if he put out the eye of a freed man (a former slave), he would pay one gold mina. If he put out the eye of a man's slave, then he would have to pay one-half of the slave's value.

Here are just some of the laws and principles set forth in Hammurabi's Code.

1. In some cases, Hammurabi's Code relied on the *River-God* to judge a case. For example, if a person accused another of a crime against him, the accused could go to the river and jump in. If he drowned, the person who accused him of the crime took possession of his house. But, if he didn't drown, it meant the River-God had decided he was innocent. The person who brought the accusation was then put to death, and the one who leaped into the river took possession of the house that had belonged to his accuser.

   Does this remind you of any type of justice that took place in the early history of our country? If so, explain.

   _____

   _____

   _____

   _____

   _____

2. The Code had specific penalties for professional men who made mistakes:

   *Judges*: If a judge tried a case and it was discovered his decision was wrong, and it was his fault, then the judge would pay twelve times the fine set by him in the case. He would be publicly removed from the judge's bench and could never render judgment again.

   *Physicians*: If a physician killed a patient or cut out a patient's eye when trying to remove a tumor, the physician would have his hands cut off.

Name _____ Date _____

*Builders*: If a builder built a house that was not sturdy and the house collapsed and killed the owner of the house, the builder was put to death. If the house collapsed and it caused the death of the owner's son, a son of the builder was put to death.

Do you think these were fair and just punishments? Explain. _____

_____

_____

_____

_____

3. A person could be put to death for stealing from a temple, receiving stolen goods from a temple, stealing the minor son of another, keeping a runaway slave and not returning him to his owner, breaking into a house and stealing, or robbery.

Were these punishments too harsh? Explain your answer. _____

_____

_____

_____

_____

4. Here is what the Code says about divorce and separation.

If a man's wife became sick and he wanted to take a second wife, he couldn't divorce his sick wife. He had to keep her and support her as long as she lived.

If a man wished to divorce his wife, he had to give back her dowry and give her the use of part of his field for farming, part of his garden, and part of his property so that she could provide for her children. When the children were grown, a portion equal to that which was given to the children was given to her. She could then marry any man she chose.

If a man wished to divorce his wife and they had no children, he had to return the purchase money and dowry and release her. If there was no purchase price, he had to give her one mina of gold as a gift.

If a woman who wished to leave her husband plunged him into debt, tried to ruin her house, or neglected her husband, she could be taken to court, and, if convicted, her husband could release her and give her nothing. If her husband did not wish to release her, he could take another wife, and the first wife was required to remain a servant in her husband's house.

If a woman wished to leave her husband, there could be a trial, and if she was not at fault and it could be proven that the husband left and neglected her, then the woman was not guilty and could take her dowry and return to her father's house. However, if she was not innocent, but left her husband and ruined her house or neglected her husband, she was thrown into the river.

Name _____ Date _____

What is your impression of the Babylonian laws regarding divorce? _____

_____

Which seemed the fairest? _____

_____

Which seemed the least fair? _____

_____

How would you compare these laws with the modern divorce laws? _____

_____

_____

_____

_____

5. Much of the Code dealt with revenge. Here are some examples.

   If a man destroyed the eye of another, his own eye would be destroyed. If a man broke the bone of another, his bone would be broken. If a man knocked out the teeth of another, his teeth would be knocked out.

   Do you think these punishments were fair? Would they work today? Why? _____

   _____

   _____

   _____

6. Here are some other unusual laws from the Code.

   If fire broke out in a house and someone who helped put out the fire stole something from the house, he was thrown into the fire.

   If conspirators met in the house of a tavern-keeper and were not captured and delivered to the court, the tavern-keeper was put to death.

   If a slave was found guilty of saying to his master, "You are not my master," his master would cut off the slave's ear.

   If a son hit his father, his hands would be cut off.

   Which of these laws is the best? Which is the worst? Why? _____

   _____

   _____

# The Statue of Zeus at Olympia

**Olympia** was a religious center and the location for many religious festivals and activities. It was a holy place with temples, monuments, and statues. Citizens of Greece would travel to Olympia to honor and worship **Zeus**, the king of the gods. Part of the festivities were athletic events that came to be known as the **Olympic Games**. But the purpose of the festivals was not the games and contests; it was the worship of Zeus, the Greeks' protector and ruler.

Over the years, the festivals became bigger and grander. Larger temples and monuments were built, and then in the fifth century B.C., a temple was built to honor Zeus. The temple was over 210 feet long and 60 feet high. There were 13 large columns on either side of the temple and six columns in the front and back. These columns supported a white marble roof. The exterior of the temple was painted and ornately decorated with sculptures depicting scenes out of **Greek mythology**. The interior was simple and unadorned. However, the statue of Zeus that was eventually erected inside was probably the most famous statue in the ancient world.

The Greek sculptor **Phidias** of Athens was to be the creator of this majestic sculpture. Phidias was a friend of **Pericles**, the ruler of **Athens**, and had been involved in building temples and statues in Athens. He was considered the best sculptor in Athens. Part of his fame was a result of the 40-foot, gold and ivory statue of **Athena** he had created to be placed in the **Parthenon.** Phidias was an obvious choice to build the statue of Zeus that would match the splendor of this remarkable temple.

Phidias depicted Zeus sitting on an elaborately carved wooden throne inset with gold, ivory, ebony, and precious stones. His feet were resting on a golden footstool. In his right hand, Zeus held a small statue of **Nike**, the goddess of victory. In his left hand he held a **scepter** with an eagle on top, which represented the power of Zeus. The construction of the statue of Zeus was likely similar to that used to produce the statue of Athena. First a framework of wood was made and then covered by plates of ivory for his skin. His clothing, beard, and hair were made of gold. His eyes were made of precious gems.

The size and lavish beauty of the statue of Zeus at Olympia was a wonder to everyone who saw it. Even enemies who invaded Greece were in awe of the statue, which remained intact for many centuries. In A.D. 394 the statue was taken to **Constantinople** and was eventually destroyed by fire. The temple that housed the Statue of Zeus was destroyed by an earthquake in the sixth century.

Name _____ Date _____

# The Statue of Zeus Quiz

Shown below are a number of sentences. Some are true and some are false. If the sentence is true, write the word "true" in front of the sentence. If the sentence is false, write a term that could replace the term written in bold type to make the sentence true.

_____ 1. The temple that housed the Statue of Zeus was destroyed by **a flood** in the sixth century.

_____ 2. **Pericles** was considered to be the king of the gods by the Greeks.

_____ 3. Olympia was an important **trading** center.

_____ 4. **Pericles** was the ruler of Athens and had been involved in building temples and statues in Athens.

_____ 5. **Phidias** of Athens was considered the best sculptor in Athens.

_____ 6. **Athena** had created a statue that was placed in the Parthenon.

_____ 7. The temple built to honor Zeus had a roof of white **marble**.

_____ 8. The right hand of the statue of Zeus held a small statue of **Adidas**, the goddess of victory.

_____ 9. In A.D. 394 the statue of Zeus was taken to **Constantinople.**

_____ 10. The statue of Zeus was eventually destroyed by **vandals**.

_____ 11. Greeks would travel to Olympia to honor and worship **Zeus**.

_____ 12. Part of the festivities at Olympia were athletic events that came to be known as the **Winter Olympics**.

_____ 13. The purpose of the festivals was not the games and contests; it was the worship of **Zeus**.

_____ 14. In the **fifth century** A.D., the temple to honor Zeus was built.

_____ 15. Enemies who invaded Greece were in such awe of the statue that they **admired** it.

_____ 16. The construction of the statue of Zeus began with a framework of **bronze**.

_____ 17. The framework of Zeus was covered by plates of **porcelain** for his skin.

_____ 18. The statue's clothing, beard, and hair were made of **Corinthian leather**.

_____ 19. The statue's eyes were made of colored **glass**.

_____ 20. Zeus was the Greeks' **protector**.

24

Name _____ Date _____

# The Greek Temples

Greek temples were rectangular buildings that had a sloping roof held by columns. There was an entrance that led into the main room where the statue of the god was displayed. Just outside this main room was an altar made of stone. Behind the main room was a smaller room where the sacred items were stored. Would you like to see what a Greek temple looked like? You probably have a picture of one in your house. You might even have one in your pocket. If you have a five dollar bill, take it out and look at the back and you will see what appears to be an ancient Greek temple. If you look at the bottom, however, you will see that it is actually a picture of the Lincoln Memorial in Washington, D.C.

Designed by architect Henry Bacon, an admirer of Greek architecture, the Lincoln Memorial was modeled after the Greek Parthenon. Bacon included 36 exterior Doric columns in the building to represent the thirty-six states in the Union when Lincoln died. The states are listed above the columns. Above those states are listed the 48 states in the Union when the memorial was constructed in 1922. Since Alaska and Hawaii were not states when the memorial was built, they are represented with a plaque on the steps.

The large statue of President Lincoln was created by Daniel Chester French. He is the same artist who created the statue of the minuteman that stands near the Old North Bridge in Concord, Massachusetts. Lincoln is shown sitting. This sitting position may well have been inspired by the statue of Zeus at Olympia, who was shown sitting on a throne, although there is no evidence to support this idea. The fact that the statue of President Lincoln takes up a large portion of the memorial is also consistent with the Greek idea of a temple. The ancient Greeks built temples to honor a god such as Zeus at Olympia or Artemis at Ephesus. It is probable that the statues of these gods occupied most of the interior.

## GREEK TEMPLES IN YOUR TOWN?

By looking at the Lincoln Memorial you have a good idea of what a Greek temple looked like. You probably have also seen many other buildings in our country that have been inspired by Greek architecture. Are there any in your city? In Washington, D.C.? In other cities?

List the names and locations of buildings you have seen, either in person or in pictures, that may have been influenced by ancient Greek architecture.

| NAME OF STRUCTURE | LOCATION |
| --- | --- |
| 1. _____ | _____ |
| 2. _____ | _____ |
| 3. _____ | _____ |
| 4. _____ | _____ |
| 5. _____ | _____ |
| 6. _____ | _____ |
| 7. _____ | _____ |
| 8. _____ | _____ |
| 9. _____ | _____ |
| 10. _____ | _____ |

Name _____ Date _____

# Research on Temples

Shown below are a number of questions. In order to find the answers, you need to do research in the library. First, answer the question, and then, list what resource you used in order to find the answer.

1.  Question: In terms of ancient Greek architecture, what does **Corinthian** mean?
    Answer: _____

    _____

    Source: _____

2.  Question: In terms of ancient Greek architecture, what does **Doric** mean?
    Answer: _____

    _____

    Source: _____

3.  Question: In terms of ancient Greek architecture, what does **Ionic** mean?
    Answer: _____

    _____

    Source: _____

4.  Question: In terms of ancient Greek architecture, what does **frieze** mean?
    Answer: _____

    _____

    Source: _____

5.  Question: What was the **Parthenon**?
    Answer: _____

    _____

    Source: _____

6.  Question: In terms of ancient Greek architecture, what does **facade** mean?
    Answer: _____

    _____

    Source: _____

7.  Question: In terms of ancient Greek architecture, what does **capital** mean?
    Answer: _____

    _____

    Source: _____

# History of the Olympic Games

Olympia was a religious center in Greece and the location for many religious festivals and activities. However, it is not because of religion that we remember Olympia today. We remember Olympia because it was there that the **Olympic Games** originated. The ancient Greeks believed that humans should develop many skills, abilities, and interests. They studied philosophy, government, art, and religion. A great deal of our modern culture can be traced back to ancient Greece. But the Greeks were just as interested in athletics as they were intellectual activities. Athletic contests were held at religious festivals and even at funerals of famous people. The Greeks believed in "a healthy mind in a healthy body." Philosophers, artists, and priests were given respect and honor, but so were athletes. Champion athletes were treated as heroes.

An athlete became a champion by participating in the many athletic games that were held in various cities in Greece. Athletic contests had always been an important part of Greek society, but the first written reference to the athletic games was to the ones held in Olympia in 776 B.C. The Olympic Games were open only to male Greeks who were free-born. A person who was free-born was not a slave. Athletes from other nations could not compete and neither could women. Women were not even allowed to watch the Games. In the ancient Olympics, there was only one winner of each event. There were no second- or third-place prizes. The winner received a crown made of olive branches, but the rewards of being an Olympic champion were much greater. When a winner returned home, there were parades and celebrations. Poems and songs were written about the champion, and often statues were carved in his likeness.

The early Olympic Games had only one event—a foot race of about 200 yards. Several years later, a second, longer race was added, and eventually the Olympics included running, jumping, wrestling, boxing, chariot races, and javelin and discus throwing. There was also an event called the **pancratium,** which was a rugged event that combined wrestling and boxing. The fighters wrapped their hands in leather, which was sometimes covered with pieces of metal. The contestants would box until one surrendered. This was an "anything goes" event, and the losers were sometimes blinded, crippled, or even killed. What made this event even more brutal was that there were no weight divisions as there are in Olympic boxing or wrestling today. The biggest, heaviest, strongest man might be matched up with the smallest, lightest fighter.

The **pentathlon** was the event most sought after by the contestants, because victory in this contest brought the most honor. The pentathlon was not a separate sport but was actually five events—running, long jumping, wrestling, and throwing the javelin and discus. The first person to win three of the five events won the pentathlon. If no one won three events, then another wrestling match was added in order to find a winner. The winner of the pentathlon was an all-around athlete.

**A discus thrower**

Athletes who were to compete in the Games at Olympia trained at home for ten months and then traveled to Olympia one month before the contest in order to train. Spectators would begin arriving about this time, as well. They would watch the athletes practice, encourage those athletes from their city-state, and reminisce about past Games. The crowd of onlookers would grow as the time for the Games approached, and they would be joined by peddlers selling everything from food to souvenirs—not much different than the modern Olympic Games.

The entire festival at Olympia lasted five days and was held in such high esteem that the entire nation focused on the event. Many of the everyday activities ceased so that the citizens could attend the Games. At the time of the original Olympics, Greece was not a unified nation, but a collection of small city-states who often fought with their neighbors. Every four years, however, wars were stopped and a truce was called so athletes could go to Olympia to compete in the Games and worship Zeus. Not only were the athletes protected during the Games, but coaches and fans also could not be attacked.

The Olympic Games lasted for five days. The athletes first needed to establish that they were indeed Greek citizens so they could participate. They had to swear to compete fairly and honestly. The judges also had to swear they would be fair, honest, and not take bribes. Then the contests would begin. The athletic events were interspersed with religious ceremonies and sacrifices to Zeus. The closing event of the Games was a race run in armor. Following the Games, a feast was held.

The Olympic Games are well-known, but Olympia was not the only Greek city that had athletic games. Athletic games were held every year in one of three cities. The **Olympic Games** and the **Pythian Games** were held once every four years. The **Nemean Games** were held every other year. Here is how it would work. There would be the Olympic Games in Olympia one year, the Nemean Games would be held at Cleonae the next, the Pythian Games would be held at Delphi the next, the Nemean Games would be held at Cleonae the next, and then the Olympic Games would be held again. The Olympic Games, however, were the oldest and most important. The games in the other cities were considered warm-up events for the Olympic Games.

In A.D. 394 the Games were officially ended by the Christian emperor of Rome, Theodosius. He felt the Games were a heathen ritual and should be stopped. The modern Olympics began in Athens in 1896. In 1924 the Games were divided into the Winter and Summer Olympics. The Winter Olympics are scheduled in January and February and feature winter sports such as skiing, skating, and hockey. The Summer Games, held in July and August, feature track and field events, as well as more modern sports such as baseball and cycling. In 1994 the Games began an alternating pattern, with the Winter Games in 1994, the Summer Games in 1996, the Winter Games again in 1998, and so on.

The Olympics today differ from the original Olympics in several ways. The original Olympics were conceived by the Greeks as a way to honor their gods; the modern Games are designed as a way of honoring athletes. The original Olympics were mainly individual events; the modern Games are often team sports. The original Olympics eventually included competition in music, speaking, and theater; the modern Games have greatly expanded the areas of competition, but it has remained an athletic event.

Name _____ Date _____

# Olympic Games Synonyms

Shown below are several words used in the explanation of the Olympic Games. Look at each word written in bold-face type, and then find the word at the right that has *almost* the same meaning. Words that have the same meaning are called synonyms. Write the synonym in the blank in front of the word in bold-face type. Then write a sentence using that synonym on the line below each group of words.

_____ 1. **culture**          A. heritage       B. style          C. philosophy

_____ 2. **intellectual**     A. spiritual      B. thoughtful     C. stylish

_____ 3. **esteem**           A. ideal          B. respect        C. wonder

_____ 4. **bribes**           A. graft          B. fines          C. wages

_____ 5. **interspersed**     A. differed       B. varied         C. mixed

_____ 6. **emperor**          A. ruler          B. hero           C. celebrity

_____ 7. **heathen**          A. irreligious    B. pious          C. sacred

_____ 8. **ritual**           A. civil          B. banquet        C. ceremony

_____ 9. **conceived**        A. courteous      B. imagined       C. akin

_____ 10. **javelin**         A. spear          B. log            C. pole

_____ 11. **discus**          A. coin           B. stone          C. disk

_____ 12. **philosophy**      A. principles     B. intention      C. design

_____ 13. **festival**        A. party          B. opportunity    C. celebration

_____ 14. **stadium**         A. arena          B. gymnasium      C. field

_____ 15. **souvenirs**       A. spectators     B. mementos       C. coins

# Strange Facts About the Early Olympics

1. The Greeks thought that the gods and ghosts of the dead enjoyed watching sporting contests.
2. Sporting events were held at religious festivals and at funerals.
3. Every four years during the Olympic Games, wars were halted so that everyone could participate.
4. Forty-thousand people attended the early Olympic Games.
5. The athletes were nude when they participated in the games. *Gymnos* is a Greek word meaning "naked." *Gymnasium* means, "where one exercises naked."
6. Women or slaves were not allowed to participate in or attend the games.
7. If a woman viewed the Olympic games, she could be pushed off of a cliff.
8. Athletes who cheated or broke the rules were fined. The money from the fines was used to build statues of the gods, which were placed in front of the stadium.
9. The winner of the chariot race was not the driver, but the owner of the horse. So it was possible for a woman to win the chariot race even though she could not attend.
10. The first Olympics had only one event, a foot race that was about 660 feet long.
11. The second event in the Olympic Games was added 52 years later. It was a race twice as long as the original race.
12. The headquarters for the Games was not in Olympia, but was located about 25 miles away in a city called Elis.
13. Pisa and Elis were two Greek city-states who went to war because each claimed to be the one who had invented the idea of the Olympic Games.
14. Cities were so proud when someone from their city won the Olympics, they would often break a hole through the city wall for the winner to enter.
15. There were no weight or size classes in the boxing contests.
16. The pancratium was a sport that combined boxing, wrestling, and judo and sometimes ended in death.
17. Once during a pancratium, one fighter began choking the other as his leg was being twisted. His leg caused him so much pain he surrendered just as his opponent died of strangulation. The dead man was proclaimed the winner.
18. When the Romans conquered the Greeks, they participated in the Olympics. Once, the Emperor of Rome, Nero, entered the chariot race. In spite of the fact that he fell out of his chariot, he was declared the winner.
19. The period from one Olympic Games to the next was called an Olympiad, and the Greeks used the term to mark time. For example, they would say that some event, such as a death or war, occurred during the third Olympiad.

# The Temple of Artemis at Ephesus

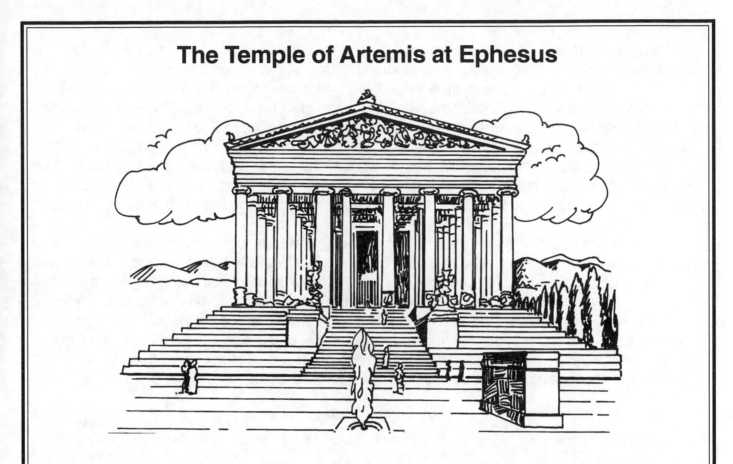

The Temple of Artemis was the largest temple of ancient times and was the first building made entirely of marble. It was built about 550 B.C. Funded by the Greek king Croesus, the temple was built in Ephesus. It was decorated in gold and featured a huge statue of the goddess Artemis, one of the twelve Olympian gods. Artemis was the twin sister of Apollo, the god of truth and light. She was the daughter of Zeus, king of the Gods, and Leto, daughter of the Elder Gods. She was considered the goddess of wild animals and the forest and a huntress. She was also associated with the Moon. While Artemis was a Greek goddess, she did not originate with the Greeks. Statues of her have been found in other countries that date back thousands of years. Her original name was Kybele, but in Egypt she was called Isis. The Arabs called her Lat, and the Romans called her Diana.

Built on a platform 430 feet by 259 feet, the rectangular temple was larger than the Parthenon in Athens and measured 366 feet by 170 feet. The huge roof was supported by over 120 elaborately carved columns. The columns were not just one solid piece of stone. Each column consisted of about 12 cylindrical blocks of marble that were raised into place with pulleys and placed on top of one another to form a column. Once the columns were in place, stonemasons cut long, rounded grooves from the top to the bottom of the column to make them more ornate. Wooden beams provided a framework that supported the roof. Inside the temple were bronze statues and paintings. There was also a room that sheltered a magnificent statue of Artemis, the goddess of the forest and the goddess of fertility. The statue was inlaid with gold, silver, and ebony.

The temple was not only a religious structure, it was a tourist attraction, meeting place, and a market. The temple was visited by merchants, tourists, and visitors who traveled to honor Artemis and to bring her offerings. The presence of the temple brought wealth to the city of Ephesus and to its artisans, who made statues and idols of the goddess. These artisans felt their livelihood was being threatened when St. Paul traveled to Ephesus to preach Christianity about A.D. 57. Christianity taught that there was only one true god and that to worship idols and statues was a sin. The merchants who produced these idols confronted St. Paul and shouted at him.

In 356 B.C. a man named Herostratus was looking for a way to have his name live on in history. He decided that if he were to destroy the beautiful temple of Artemis, then people would remember him forever. So he set fire to the temple, and it was destroyed. The roof fell to the ground and the columns were knocked over. Herostratus had secured his place in the history books.

The temple was eventually rebuilt by Alexander the Great who conquered Ephesus. The Temple of Artemis was restored to its former beauty. The reconstructed temple lasted for many years but was looted by the Goths and then flooded. By A.D. 262 the temple had been destroyed beyond repair.

There is one question that is often asked regarding the Temple of Artemis at Ephesus. "Why was it considered one of the Seven Wonders of the Ancient World?" After all, it was just a temple, and there were many temples throughout Greece. The answer to this question is given by Philon of Byzantium, who is also credited with compiling the list of the Seven Wonders of the Ancient World. He said, "I have seen the walls and Hanging Gardens of ancient Babylon, the statue of Olympian Zeus, the Colossus of Rhodes, the mighty work of the high Pyramids, and the tomb of Mausolus. But when I saw the sacred house of Artemis that towers to the clouds, the other wonders were placed in the shade, for the Sun himself has never looked upon its equal outside Olympus."

## A GREEK TEMPLE

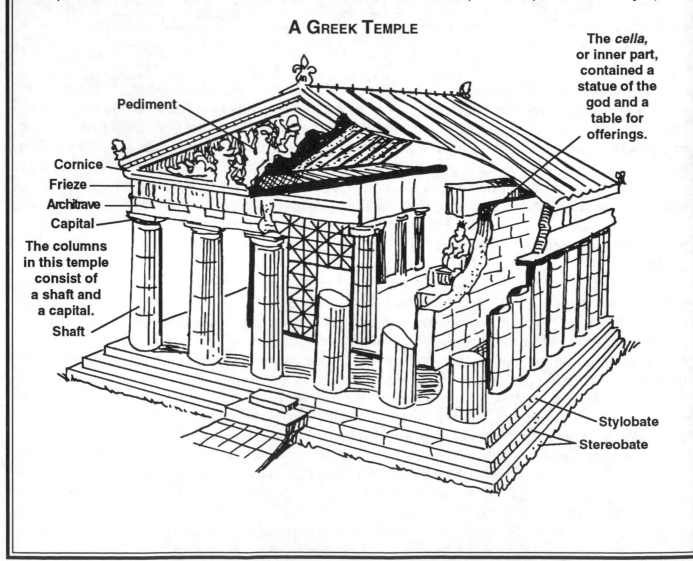

Pediment

The *cella,* or inner part, contained a statue of the god and a table for offerings.

Cornice
Frieze
Architrave
Capital

The columns in this temple consist of a shaft and a capital.

Shaft

Stylobate
Stereobate

Name _____ Date _____

# The Temple of Artemis at Ephesus Quiz

Shown below are a number of sentences. Some are true and some are false. If the sentence is true, write the word "true" in front of the sentence. If the sentence is false, write a term that could replace the bold term to make the sentence true.

_____ 1. The Roman name for Artemis was **Diana**.

_____ 2. Artemis was the twin sister of **Apollo**, the god of truth and light.

_____ 3. Artemis was considered the goddess of wild **parties.**

_____ 4. The Temple of **Artemis** was the largest temple of ancient times.

_____ 5. The Greek king **Aristotle** funded the building of the Temple of Artemis.

_____ 6. The Temple of Artemis was the largest temple of ancient times and was the first building made entirely of **marbles**.

_____ 7. The temple was built in **Ephesus**.

_____ 8. **Wooden** beams were used to provide the framework for the roof.

_____ 9. **St. Luke** traveled to Ephesus to preach Christianity about A.D. 57.

_____ 10. **Zeus** was the father of Artemis.

_____ 11. **Leno** was the mother of Artemis.

_____ 12. There were over 120 elaborately carved **columns** supporting the roof of the temple.

_____ 13. Each column consisted of about 12 cylindrical blocks of **bronze.**

_____ 14. Each column piece was raised into place with **pulleys** and placed on top of one another to form a column.

_____ 15. The temple was **smaller** than the Parthenon.

_____ 16. In 356 B.C. a man named **Herostratus** burned the Temple of Artemis so that people would remember his name forever.

_____ 17. The temple was eventually rebuilt by **Julius Caeser** who conquered Ephesus.

_____ 18. The reconstructed temple was looted by the **Goths**.

_____ 19. The temple was flooded, and by A.D. **262** it had been destroyed beyond repair.

_____ 20. The presence of the temple brought wealth to **Athens** and to its artisans, who made statues and idols of the goddess Artemis.

Name _____ Date _____

# Research on Greek Life

    Shown below are a number of questions. In order to find the answer, you need to do research in the library. First answer the question, and then list what resource you used in order to find the answer.

1. Question: What was the **Acropolis**?

   Answer: _____

   _____

   Source: _____

2. Question: What was the **agora**?

   Answer: _____

   _____

   Source: _____

3. Question: What was **ostracism**?

   Answer: _____

   _____

   Source: _____

4. Question: What were **demi-gods**?

   Answer: _____

   _____

   Source: _____

5. Question: What was **epic poetry**?

   Answer: _____

   _____

   Source: _____

6. Question: What was an **oracle**?

   Answer: _____

   _____

   Source: _____

7. Question: What was a **polis**?

   Answer: _____

   _____

   Source: _____

Name _____  Date _____

# Temple of Artemis Word Search

Find the words listed below in the word search puzzle. They are all related to the Temple of Artemis in some way. Words may be printed in the puzzle forward, backward, horizontally, vertically, or diagonally.

```
I  W  Y  H  O  V  L  S  M  T  G  O  T  H  S  F  M  A  V  L
S  S  T  E  V  K  V  T  A  H  T  E  H  O  N  B  X  X  Z  E
C  G  I  P  O  H  W  V  R  F  J  K  O  Z  T  K  G  D  R  T
O  X  N  H  Q  P  F  B  D  P  W  B  H  A  U  Y  O  L  H  O
L  J  A  E  W  O  S  W  A  J  Q  L  X  G  C  B  D  U  S  W
U  J  I  S  R  E  Z  J  O  Z  Y  Y  D  X  O  E  D  A  M  E
M  B  T  U  H  E  F  Z  M  Q  O  N  Q  K  R  L  E  P  W  F
N  L  S  S  I  A  R  T  E  M  I  S  O  F  J  E  S  T  C  N
S  A  I  E  S  M  K  Q  P  U  O  Z  U  B  U  E  S  S  T  I
U  U  R  O  P  J  B  S  J  C  S  W  M  R  E  D  Y  Z  W  X
T  W  H  I  C  M  G  R  W  A  P  O  L  L  O  F  L  S  G  P
A  A  C  T  O  P  E  F  R  R  E  T  E  B  R  S  H  G  V  H
R  U  R  M  Y  V  V  S  N  O  S  A  M  E  N  O  T  S  E  U
T  D  D  T  L  Q  H  S  V  Y  W  M  D  A  U  J  X  P  L  N
S  L  Y  I  I  H  X  Z  E  J  O  N  N  K  Z  I  L  Y  E  T
O  O  S  D  E  S  W  L  H  O  A  A  P  P  V  D  Q  K  L  R
R  G  T  R  I  D  A  H  N  X  I  C  R  O  E  S  U  S  B  E
E  Y  V  A  C  S  U  N  E  D  P  Y  N  J  U  E  O  O  R  S
H  C  X  E  L  Y  I  L  S  T  H  V  M  P  W  R  P  Q  A  S
G  O  E  O  P  I  A  S  V  E  L  U  Q  I  L  W  Q  R  M  U
```

## WORD LIST

| | | |
|---|---|---|
| ALEXANDER | APOLLO | ARTEMIS |
| ARTISANS | CHRISTIANITY | COLUMNS |
| CROESUS | DIANA | EBONY |
| EPHESUS | GODDESS | GOLD |
| GOTHS | HEROSTRATUS | HUNTRESS |
| ISIS | KYBELE | LAT |
| LETO | MARBLE | MOON |
| SILVER | STONEMASONS | ST. PAUL |
| ZEUS | | |

Name _____ Date _____

# Greek and Roman Gods

Religion was an important element of ancient Greek life. Two of the Seven Wonders of the Ancient World were tributes to Greek gods. The Statue of Zeus at Olympia was a tribute to the ruler of the gods, Zeus. The Temple of Artemis at Ephesus was built in honor of Zeus' daughter, Artemis, the huntress. One of the mistakes some people make is to confuse Greek gods with Roman gods.

Using the list at the bottom of the page, place the appropriate Greek god to the left of the attributes that describe each. Then in the blank on the right, write the name of the corresponding Roman god or goddess.

| | Greek God | Attributes | Roman God |
|---|---|---|---|
| 1. | _____ | God of the Sea | _____ |
| 2. | _____ | God of Love | _____ |
| 3. | _____ | God of War | _____ |
| 4. | _____ | Goddess of the Hearth | _____ |
| 5. | _____ | Goddess of Wild Animals, the Hunt, and the Moon | _____ |
| 6. | _____ | Goddess of Cities, Arts, Industry, Wisdom, and War | _____ |
| 7. | _____ | Goddess of the Corn or Harvest | _____ |
| 8. | _____ | God of the Underworld | _____ |
| 9. | _____ | Goddess of Love | _____ |
| 10. | _____ | God of the Smith | _____ |
| 11. | _____ | Queen of the Gods | _____ |
| 12. | _____ | Ruler of the Gods | _____ |
| 13. | _____ | Hero Noted for His Strength and Courage | _____ |
| 14. | _____ | Maiden of the Spring | _____ |
| 15. | _____ | Messenger of the Gods | _____ |
| 16. | _____ | God of Sleep | _____ |
| 17. | _____ | Ruler of the Titans | _____ |
| 18. | _____ | A Hero and Traveler | _____ |
| 19. | _____ | The Goat God | _____ |
| 20. | _____ | God of Wine and Revelry | _____ |

**Greek Gods**

Aphrodite; Ares; Artemis; Athena; Demeter; Dionysus; Eros; Hades; Hephaistos; Hera; Herakles; Hermes; Hestia; Hypnos; Kronos; Odysseus; Pan; Persephone; Poseidon; Zeus

**Roman Gods**

Bacchus; Ceres; Cupid; Diana; Faunus; Hercules; Juno; Jupiter; Mars; Mercury; Minerva; Neptune; Pluto; Proserpina; Saturn; Somnus; Ulysses; Venus; Vesta; Vulcan

Name _____ Date _____

# Greek Gods and Goddesses from A to Z

The column at the left lists key words associated with Greek gods or goddesses. Write the appropriate name of the Greek deity on the blanks opposite the word. Once you have finished, you will see that the letters in the circles spell out a phrase. Write that phrase at the bottom of the page.

1. A snake-headed Medusa
2. Son of Zeus, Brother to Artemis
3. The Goddess of Hate
4. The Archer of Love
5. The Goat God
6. Known as the Furies
7. A Mother to Aphrodite
8. Three Beautiful Sister Goddesses
9. The Sun God
10. God of the Underworld
11. The Gorgon
12. Wife of Herakles in Olympus
13. God of Sea
14. Goddess of the Hunt
15. Queen of Olympus
16. God of the Smith
17. Offspring of Zeus and Themis
18. God of War
19. God of Sleep
20. Messenger of the Gods
21. A Strong and Brave Hero
22. Goddess of the Hearth
23. Lord of the Titans
24. King of Gods

25. Phrase:_____

**Use these words:** Apollo, Artemis, Ares, Dione, Erida, Erinyes, Eros, Fates, Gorgon, Graces, Hades, Hebe, Helios, Hera, Herakles, Hermes, Hestia, Hephaistos, Hypnos, Kronos, Medusa, Pan, Poseidon, Zeus

Name _____ Date _____

# Creating a Greek God or Goddess

In ancient Greece the people believed that the gods and goddesses lived in a beautiful palace so high on Mount Olympus that it could not be seen by humans. It was thought that they had many human qualities such as love, hate, anger, and jealousy, but they were immortal, which means they lived forever. In ancient Greece there was a god who ruled every aspect of life. Ares was the god of war, Apollo was the god of music, Athena was the goddess of learning, and so on. In addition, there were stories about each of the gods that told how they were born, who their parents were, and what activities they participated in. Here is an example of Artemis, for whom the temple was built at Ephesus.

**Name**: Artemis

**Goddess of:** She was considered the goddess of wild animals and the forest and a huntress. She hunted with silver arrows and protected children, pregnant women, and baby animals. She was also associated with the Moon.

**Family:** Father was Zeus, mother was Leto, and her twin brother was Apollo.

**Personality:** Artemis was strong and brave. She loved animals, but she was often cold and without pity.

**A Story About Artemis**: One night a young hunter named Actaeon happened on a pool where Artemis and her nymphs were bathing. Instead of leaving, he watched. When Artemis saw Actaeon watching, she threw a handful of water on him, turning him into a stag. Actaeon's hounds immediately leaped on him, and since he was unable to call them off, they killed him.

It is apparent that the stories about the Greek gods and goddesses grew out of the life and interest of the citizens in ancient Greece. They were appropriate for their time. If the gods and goddesses who lived on Mount Olympus would have been created today, in our time, how might they be different?

Your assignment is to create an ancient Greek god or goddess just as the ancient Greeks did. The difference is you are creating him or her today. What would the god's or goddess' name be? What would he or she rule? Use your imagination and fill in the following information on the god or goddess you create. Use the back of this page or your own paper if you need more space.

**Name:** _____

**God or Goddess of:** _____

**Family:** _____

**Personality:** _____

_____

**A Story Involving God or Goddess:** _____

_____

_____

_____

_____

_____

# The Mausoleum at Halicarnassus

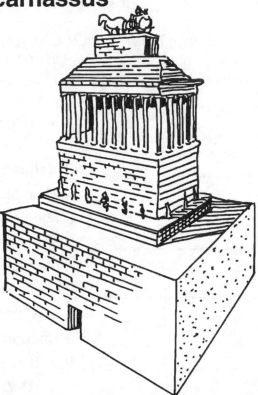

Not far from Ephesus, the site of the Temple of Artemis, was **Halicarnassus**, the capital city of **Caria**. Caria was part of the **Persian Empire** and is located in an area that is now Turkey. In the fourth century B.C., Persia controlled Asia Minor, Egypt, Syria, Mesopotamia, and parts of India. Since Persia was located so far from some of these areas, many were actually ruled by local governors. The King of Caria was a man known as **Mausolus**, the son of a governor who had ruled on behalf of the Persians. Mausolus ruled from 377 B.C. until his death in 353 B.C. When Mausolous succeeded his father as governor, he expanded his rule over most of southwestern Asia. Even though Mausolus and his father both acknowledged Persia as their rulers, they really had very little contact with this distant conqueror.

Mausolus was an ambitious ruler who was able to unite many Greek city-states and he spent much of his reign as governor improving the capital city, Halicarnassus. He built temples and shrines and made other improvements that made Halicarnassus a beautiful and prosperous city. One of the most lavish improvements to the capital was a beautiful palace he had built for himself and his queen.

Mausolus was married to **Artemisia,** who was named after the Greek goddess Artemis, the goddess of wild things and fertility. Artemisia was not only Mausolus' wife, but she was also his sister. It sounds strange today for a man to marry his own sister, but in Caria, it was expected that the ruler should do this. Near the end of his life, Mausolus decided to build a monument to himself, so that after he died, he would be remembered. Construction began, but Mausolus died before the tomb was finished. His wife, Artemisia, hired the best architects, sculptors, and stonemasons to complete the royal tomb for her husband. Unfortunately, Artemisia also died before the tomb was built, but the workers and artists continued their project until it was finished. The tomb was so magnificent that today we call any large, beautiful tomb a **mausoleum**.

One is tempted to compare the tomb of Mausolus to the pyramids, since both were built as tombs to bury rulers. But they were quite different. The Great Pyramid was renown for its size, while the tomb of Mausolus was renown for its beauty. The tomb consisted of three levels. The base, or bottom part, of the mausoleum measured 126 feet by 105 feet. It was the burial chamber for Mausolus and Artemisa. A row of lion statues was placed along the top edges of the base to protect the burial chamber. The second level was smaller and placed above the first level. Surrounding the second level were elaborately carved statues of gods, goddesses, and warriors. The third level was built like a Greek temple, with columns and statues. The columns supported the roof, which was shaped like a pyramid. The pyramid was not smooth but was like steps that led up to the top of the mausoleum, which displayed a ten-foot statue of the King and Queen in a horse-drawn chariot. The tomb rose 140 feet high.

The mausoleum remained intact for 16 centuries, but it was eventually destroyed by an earthquake and then torn apart so the stones could be used for other building projects.

Name _____ Date _____

# The Mausoleum at Halicarnassus Quiz

Shown below are a number of sentences. Some are true and some are false. If the sentence is true, write the word "true" in front of the sentence. If the sentence is false, write a term that could replace the term written in bold type to make the sentence true.

_____ 1. Mausolus united many **Roman** city-states.

_____ 2. Mausolus was the **president** of Caria.

_____ 3. **Halicarnassus** was a beautiful and prosperous city.

_____ 4. Mausolus was married to **Artemisia.**

_____ 5. Mausolus was married to his **cousin**.

_____ 6. **Greece** controlled Asia Minor, Egypt, Syria, Mesopotamia, and parts of India.

_____ 7. Caria was part of the Persian Empire and is located in an area that is now **Turkey**.

_____ 8. **Halicarnassus** was the capital city of Caria.

_____ 9. Mausolus was the **nephew** of a governor who had ruled on behalf of the Persians.

_____ 10. Halicarnassus, the capital city of Caria, was located near **Athens**, the site of the Temple of Artemis.

_____ 11. The tomb built to bury Mausolus was famous for its **size**.

_____ 12. The tomb was so impressive that today we call any large, beautiful tomb a **mausoleum**.

_____ 13. The tomb consisted of **three** levels.

_____ 14. The base, or bottom part, of the mausoleum was the **living** chamber for Mausolus and Artemisa.

_____ 15. Surrounding the second level were elaborately carved statues of gods and **athletes**.

_____ 16. The third level was built like a **Greek** temple, with columns and statues.

_____ 17. The top of the mausoleum displayed a ten-foot statue of the **King and Queen** in a horse-drawn chariot.

_____ 18. The mausoleum remained intact for sixteen **years**.

_____ 19. The mausoleum was eventually destroyed by an **earthquake**.

_____ 20. The stones from the destroyed mausoleum were eventually **sold as souvenirs**.

# Burial and Death

It seems that humans spend as much time thinking of death and the afterlife as they do thinking about the present. Two of the Seven Wonders of the Ancient World were tombs—the Great Pyramid at Giza and the Mausoleum at Halicarnassus. Other magnificent buildings have also been built as tombs. The Taj Mahal in India as well as many grand tombs for ancient Chinese emperors have caused visitors to marvel at their beauty and architecture.

Humans may well be the only creatures to acknowledge death. Certainly burying the dead and performing elaborate and religious ceremonies over the deceased is something that only humans do. It is a practice performed by almost all cultures long before recorded history. Burial rites and customs have varied throughout history and cultures, but most seem to have been performed for the purpose of honoring the dead or the gods. Some rites were devised so that the deceased would be able to have the items needed for his or her existence in the afterlife.

The ancient Egyptians believed that if a person's body was preserved on earth, the soul would have eternal life in the kingdom of Osiris, their god, so they developed an embalming method known as mummification to preserve the body of the deceased. When the mummy was placed in the tomb, a priest would perform a ritual called "Opening of the Mouth." A priest would touch the mummy's mouth with a special instrument that was intended to enable the deceased to control his body again. The mummy was then placed in its tomb along with clay pots of food and water and other possessions that could be used in the afterlife.

The Greeks believed that, when they died, their souls would be ferried across a river. They put a coin in the mouth of each corpse as payment to the ferryman. Some of these customs were observed and adopted by the Romans. The Romans, in turn, brought their customs of funeral ceremonies to other countries as they invaded. In short, while each civilization developed its own custom for dealing with death, each was aware of and adopted some of the customs of past civilizations.

**The Egyptian "Opening of the Mouth" ceremony**

Name _____ Date _____

# Burial and Death Terms

Throughout the ages, a vocabulary to accompany this fascination with death has been developed. How well do you understand the following terms dealing with death and burial? Below and to the right are a number of definitions. In the blank before each definition, write the word that is described by the definition. Choose from the terms given below.

**TERM**                                              **DEFINITION**

_____ 1. Originally a Roman underground burial ground, the term now refers to any underground burial ground with walking space, including the basements of mausoleums.

_____ 2. A furnace or facility for the incineration of corpses.

_____ 3. A vehicle that carries a coffin to a church or cemetery.

_____ 4. A stand on which the coffin is placed.

_____ 5. A structure or sculpture placed as a memorial for one who has died.

_____ 6. A method of embalming and preserving a dead person or animal. This method was used by ancient Egyptians.

_____ 7. Named after King Mausolus, the term now refers to a large, stately tomb.

_____ 8. This means an empty tomb. It is a monument erected in honor of a dead person who is buried somewhere else.

_____ 9. A term often connected with Egyptian mummies, it is a stone coffin.

_____ 10. A watch or vigil over the body of a deceased person before burial. It is sometimes accompanied by feasting and drinking.

_____ 11. An underground vault or chamber, usually beneath a church, used as a burial place.

_____ 12. Where dead bodies are kept before burial or cremation, usually a funeral home. They also sell coffins.

_____ 13. A cloth that is used to cover a body for burial.

_____ 14. A dead body.

_____ 15. A cemetery for Native Americans.

_____ 16. The box in which a corpse is buried.

_____ 17. A graveyard. A place to bury the dead.

_____ 18. An inscription placed on a tombstone.

_____ 19. A speech or written praise of someone who has died.

_____ 20. To treat the deceased with preservatives in order to prevent decay.

_____ 21. One who arranges for the burial or cremation. Sometimes called a funeral director or undertaker.

_____ 22. One who grieves for someone who dies.

**Use these words:** bier, burial ground, catacombs, cemetery, cenotaph, coffin, corpse, crematorium, crypt, embalm, epitaph, eulogy, hearse, mausoleum, monument, mortician, mortuary, mourner, mummification, sarcophagus, shroud, wake

Name _____ Date _____

# It's Greek to Me Crossword Puzzle

Literally thousands of English words have been derived from the Greek language. Here is a crossword puzzle that uses just a fraction of the words taken from this incredible culture. Use the clues below to complete the puzzle.

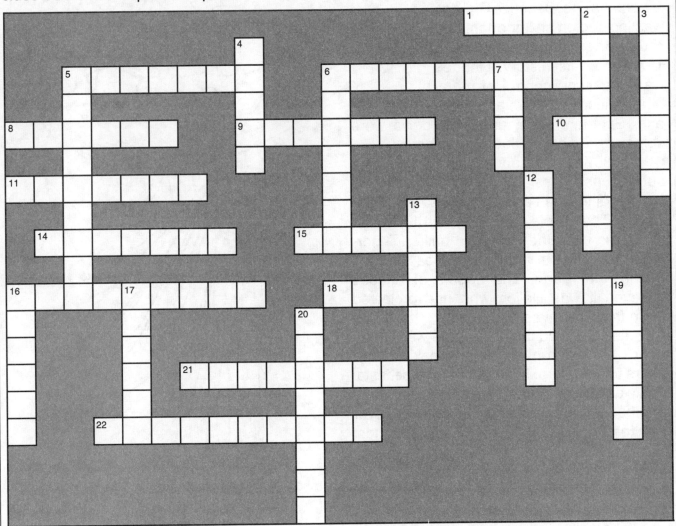

**ACROSS**

1. One of a series of events
5. The study of how words form sentences
6. Stops the growth of germs
8. A humorous play
9. A sole ruler, such as a king
10. A brave person who has risked his or her life
11. A play in which the main character suffers
14. The study of life and of living organisms
15. A cruel ruler
16. Government by the people
18. The science of using numbers and symbols to explain measurement and quantities
21. The mathematics of measurement and relationships of points, lines, angles, surfaces, and solids
22. The study of the nature of things based on logic

**DOWN**

2. A group of musicians who play together on various types of instruments
3. The study of the relationship between living things and the environment
4. A play
5. A room or building designed for indoor sports
6. A school
7. One who writes poetry
12. Tactics involved in managing government
13. This keeps a ship from drifting
16. A dictator
17. A building for worship
19. An institution designed for learning
20. An actor or actress

# The Colossus of Rhodes

Rhodes was an island in the Mediterranean close to where Turkey is located today. On this small island were three Greek city-states that were united in 408 B.C. to become one. Because Rhodes was located on an important sea route, the island prospered. Throughout its history, Rhodes was under the control of many other nations or city-states. Athens, Sparta, Persia, and Macedonia were some of the nations that ruled Rhodes.

In 307 B.C., Macedonia attacked Rhodes but was unsuccessful. When the Macedonians retreated, they left a lot of military equipment behind. The people of Rhodes sold this equipment and used the money to build an enormous statue of their sun god, Helios, the main god of the island. The people of Rhodes believed it was Helios who had protected them from the invasion.

It is believed that the statue was begun after the invasion in 304 B.C. and took about 12 years to complete. It sat on a stone pedestal that was 50 feet high. The statue itself rose to another 110 feet and probably weighed over 300 tons. The statue was not solid like most statues of the period, but was a framework, or skeleton, of iron with a skin of bronze. Stones were placed inside the framework to add stability to the hollow statue.

The white marble pedestal was built first, and then stone columns were built, and iron rods were sunk into the columns to form and shape the statue. The bronze plates that made up the skin of the statue were formed on the ground in sections and then lifted into place and attached to the iron framework. The builders used the same technique that was used by the builders of the pyramids to raise the heavy bronze plates to the upper levels of the statue. As they attached the bronze plates and finished the lower levels of the statue, they built a ramp of earth around the structure so that they could carry the plates up the ramp and put them in place. After each level was finished, the ramp was made higher until builders were working on the head of the statue and the rest was completely covered by earth. Once the head was finished, the dirt was removed, the bronze skin was polished, and the statue was completed.

No one knows where the statue was placed on the island. For many years people thought that the statue actually straddled the harbor with one foot placed on one shore and the other placed on the opposite shore. The belief was that the ships would then enter the harbor by sailing underneath the legs of the Colossus. Most historians no longer believe this. The Colossus may have been close to the harbor, or it might have been further inland.

What the statue looked like is also a mystery. However, since we know that the Colossus was cast in the image of Helios, the sun god, and we have sculptures and coins that show how the people thought Helios looked, we can guess how the huge statue might have appeared. Helios is usually shown with long hair, without a beard, and with a crown of spiked rays on his head, similar to the Statue of Liberty. People have theorized that the statue may have held a container of fire and acted as a lighthouse. Others feel the statue's arm may have been extended, as if to welcome visitors. However, many sculptors depicted Helios as nude, a cloak over his left arm and his right hand shading his eyes. This may very well be how the Colossus appeared.

About 50 years after the Colossus of Rhodes was completed, an earthquake broke the statue off at the knees, and the ruins lay on the ground for many centuries. There was an offer to rebuild the statue, but an oracle said that it should not be rebuilt. In ancient Greece, an oracle was a priest or priestess who was able to talk to a god in order to answer people's questions about the future or other important matters.

Even the ruins of the Colossus of Rhodes were a source of wonder because of their size and engineering achievement. People traveled to Rhodes just to look at the fallen statue. Eventually, invaders took the pieces of the broken Colossus to Syria, where it was melted down and used to produce other items.

Although the Colossus of Rhodes only lasted about 50 years, it has served as a source of inspiration for many artists. A study of the Statue of Liberty by the French sculptor, Auguste Bartholdi, will reveal that his creation was similar to the Colossus. The building technique of a hollow metal frame covered by metal plates was used in both statues. Both were about the same size, and both were placed near a harbor. Even the appearances of the two statues are strikingly similar, including a crown of spiked sun rays.

Name _____ Date _____

# The Colossus of Rhodes Quiz

Shown below are a number of sentences. Some are true and some are false. If the sentence is true, write the word "true" in front of the sentence. If the sentence is false, write a term that could replace the bold term to make the sentence true.

_____ 1. The statue at Rhodes was called the **Colossus** because of its huge size.

_____ 2. Rhodes was an island in the **Baltic** Sea.

_____ 3. Rhodes is close to where **Turkey** is located today.

_____ 4. The people of Rhodes sold discarded **military** equipment and used the money to build an enormous statue.

_____ 5. The people of Rhodes believed it was **Helios** who had protected them from the invasion, so they built a statue of him.

_____ 6. Helios was the **Moon** god, the main god of the island.

_____ 7. Rhodes was a **Greek** city-state.

_____ 8. The statue took about **120** years to complete.

_____ 9. The statue sat on a stone pedestal that was **50** feet high.

_____ 10. The statue rose **110** feet above the pedestal.

_____ 11. The statue weighed over **300** tons.

_____ 12. **Steel** rods were sunk into the columns to form and shape the statue.

_____ 13. **Copper** plates were used to make the skin of the statue.

_____ 14. The statue only lasted for about **50** years.

_____ 15. The statue was destroyed by **fire**.

_____ 16. **Metal pieces** were placed inside to add stability to the hollow statue.

_____ 17. Someone offered to rebuild the statue, but the **king** said that it should not be rebuilt.

_____ 18. An **oracle** was a priest or priestess who was able to talk to a god.

_____ 19. The ruins, which lay on the ground for many centuries, were a source of wonder because of their size and **engineering**.

_____ 20. The broken Colossus was eventually taken to **Greece**, where it was melted down and used to produce other items.

Name _____ Date _____

# Research on Greek Warfare

The armed attack that Rhodes experienced was not uncommon. In ancient times, communities evolved and were independent. These independent communities were called city-states, although most of them were quite small. The competition between the individual city-states was apparent in the Olympic Games and other kinds of endeavors. Sometimes the competition was so intense it erupted into a war. Young men felt a great allegiance to their city-state and were happy to defend it by becoming soldiers. Those wealthy enough to own a horse fought in the cavalry. Those who could afford armor fought as armed soldiers. Poor citizens were archers or used slings to toss stones.

1.  Question: What were the **hoplites**?

    Answer: _____

    _____

    Source: _____

2.  Question: What were **hopla**?

    Answer: _____

    _____

    Source: _____

3.  Question: What was **the Peloponnesian War**?

    Answer: _____

    _____

    Source: _____

4.  Question: What was **the Battle of Marathon**?

    Answer: _____

    _____

    Source: _____

5.  Question: What was **the Trojan War**?

    Answer: _____

    _____

    Source: _____

6.  Question: What was a **phalanx**?

    Answer: _____

    _____

    Source: _____

# The Lighthouse of Alexandria

The first of the Seven Wonders of the Ancient World was the Great Pyramid in Giza, Egypt. The last of the Seven Wonders was also built in Egypt 2,300 years later. It was known as the Pharos of Alexandria. The time span between the construction of these two structures represents about half of recorded history. Even before recorded history, people began putting lights along the coast in order to guide sailors at night. They began by simply building huge fires on the cliffs overlooking the ocean. Eventually, these fires were placed on stones so that they could be seen more easily. More and more stones were used until the fires sat high on a stone tower. This is how the idea of a lighthouse was born.

The first, tallest, and most magnificent lighthouse in history was built outside the harbor of Alexandria, Egypt in 279 B.C. It was built on a small island named Pharos in the Mediterranean Sea. The lighthouse was called "Pharos" after the island on which it was placed and became so well-known that the word "pharos" means lighthouse in many languages. The Pharos of Alexandria was different from all of the other Seven Wonders of the Ancient World. It was not only beautiful and an architectural marvel, it served an important function for the city. It provided sailors a beacon to guide them to a safe return to the harbor. The lighthouse was built so well that it lasted about 1,500 years.

The idea for the lighthouse originated with Alexander the Great. As the Macedonian conqueror extended his far-reaching empire, he named many cities after himself. Most no longer exist, but one that he not only named after himself, but founded as well, is Alexandria, Egypt. While sailing on the Nile River one day, he saw a site west of the Nile's mouth that he felt would be a good location for a city. He stopped and told his men how he wanted the city laid out. The city was designed with areas for palaces, parks, and gardens. Alexander also wanted a lighthouse to safely guide sailors through the double harbor to the city. Alexander died before the city was built. Ptolemy Soter succeeded Alexander, and after Alexandria was completed, he ordered the lighthouse to be built. He too died before the lighthouse was completed. His son, Ptolemy II, completed the project.

The lighthouse consisted of three parts. The lowest section was rectangular and measured a little over 180 feet in height. This section had a cylindrical core with a circular ramp that led to the top of the lighthouse. Around the ramp, along the outer walls of the section, were rooms where the soldiers and workers lived. Just above the rectangular section was an octagonal-shaped section that was about 90 feet high. This section was smaller than the first and only housed the circular ramp to the top. The top section of the lighthouse was about 24 feet high and shaped like a cylinder. It was here that the fire that guided the sailors to safety burned. On the top of the lighthouse was a statue of a Greek god. The total height of the lighthouse, including the base, was about 384 feet.

An outstanding feature of the lighthouse was how far the light could be seen. It was recorded that the light could be seen for almost 35 miles out at sea. This remarkable technological accomplishment was possible because of the mirror that was used to reflect the light. The mirror was used to reflect sunlight during the day and the light from a fire at night. According to folklore, the mirror was so strong it could even be used to burn enemy ships as they approached Alexandria. It is likely that the mirror was made of polished brass.

In the twelfth century A.D., the lighthouse was no longer needed because the harbor had become filled with silt , so the lighthouse was not taken care of. It was toppled by an earthquake in the fourteenth century, and the ruins were eventually used for other building projects.

At the top of the lighthouse was a statue of a Greek god. Some believe it was a statue of Zeus, the king of the gods. Others believe it was Helios, the god of the Sun. Still others think that it may have been Poseidon, the god of the sea.

The fire in the top section of the lighthouse provided the light to guide sailors. The light was made more intense by being reflected by an enormous mirror. Some writers have suggested that the mirror was made of glass, but it was probably made of polished brass.

A ramp led from the base and circled its way upward to the top. The workers used this ramp to drive horse-drawn wagons with fuel to the top of the second level. The fuel was raised to the top through a shaft by pulleys.

Surrounding the ramp at the lower level were hundreds of rooms provided for soldiers, workers, and horses. Each room had a window so that ships could be observed as they approached Alexandria.

There was a wall around the lighthouse that protected the building from the sea. The wall, the platform on which it stood, and the lighthouse itself were not made with ordinary mortar joining the stones. Melted lead was used to make the structure safe from the pounding waves.

Name _____ Date _____

# The Lighthouse of Alexandria Quiz

Shown below are a number of sentences. Some are true and some are false. If the sentence is true, write the word "true" in front of the sentence. If the sentence is false, write a term that could replace the bold term to make the sentence true.

_____ 1. The idea for the lighthouse at Alexandria originated with **Alexander the Great**.

_____ 2. Surrounding the ramp at the lower level of the lighthouse were hundreds of rooms for **travelers.**

_____ 3. **An elevator** led from the base to the top.

_____ 4. The **Lighthouse at Alexandria** was the tallest and most magnificent lighthouse in history.

_____ 5. On the top of the lighthouse was a statue of **Alexander**.

_____ 6. Of the Seven Wonders of the Ancient World, the **Lighthouse at Alexandria** was the only one that had a practical use for the city.

_____ 7. The purpose of the lighthouse at Alexandria was to guide sailors to the **harbor**.

_____ 8. The lighthouse was located on a small island called **Corsica**.

_____ 9. Because of the lighthouse's location, the word **Corsica** means lighthouse in many countries.

_____ 10. The lighthouse was destroyed by **Napoleon**.

_____ 11. Of the Seven Wonders of the Ancient World, the **Lighthouse at Alexandria** was the last built.

_____ 12. Alexandria was named after **Alexander Hamilton**.

_____ 13. An outstanding feature of the lighthouse was how far the **light** could be seen.

_____ 14. The mirror was used to reflected **sunlight** during the day.

_____ 15. It is likely that the mirror was made of polished **silver**.

_____ 16. There was a wall around the lighthouse that protected the building from the **sea**.

_____ 17. Instead of mortar, melted **lead** was used to join the stones of the wall.

_____ 18. The lowest section of the lighthouse was **round**.

_____ 19. The section just above the lowest was shaped like an **octagon**.

_____ 20. The top section of the lighthouse was shaped like a **pyramid**.

# Trading and Lighthouses

By 2000 B.C., people were aware of civilizations far from their own countries. They learned about Egypt, Mesopotamia, and India. They learned that these other countries produced goods they did not. Sometimes the goods these other countries produced were foods that could not be grown in their native land or items of practical or decorative value to be used in their homes or temples. This is how trade among countries began.

Two problems had to be solved when countries began to trade with one another. First, since there was no coin money, how could goods be purchased? This problem was solved by **barter**. Countries swapped goods for goods, or they swapped goods for precious metals. The second problem they needed to solve was how to get the goods from one city or country to the other. In ancient times, cities were separated by great distances. Certainly there were roads, but they were hardly more than primitive paths that went over hills, mountains, streams, and rivers. In addition, the carts used to carry goods from city to city were crudely made, held very little, and required a great deal of power, either human or animal, to move. Ships, on the other hand, could hold an enormous amount of goods while sails and wind provided the power to carry these goods to distant ports. With the solution of these problems, trade among countries increased.

Trading became a profitable and favorite profession. Greek ships would leave a port filled with wine, olives, honey, and wool, and they would return with spices, ivory, gold, and grain. Each trading ship that entered the harbor was the topic of conversation throughout the city. The markets where the merchants sold their goods were opened up to foreigners as well as citizens.

Trading ships, or freighters, were not the only kind of ships that were developed. These ships were large and were perfect for transporting goods, but they were not so good for war. War ships were slim vessels designed to sail faster than trading ships. Trading ships relied on huge sails, but war ships also used oars to add power and speed. Galley slaves were used to pull the oars, and there was a bronze battering ram on the front of the ship to ram and sink enemy ships. The Greek war ship, a **galley**, was fast and deadly. It was also called a **trireme** because there were three banks of oars on each side of the ship.

While the Greeks were excellent sailors and could navigate by the stars, the Sun, and the Moon, they usually sailed their ships close to the shore, relying on landmarks to guide them. Lighthouses served this function well. Not only could sailors use the lighthouse in order to decide where they were, but the lighthouse could also guide them past rocky reefs into a safe harbor. The lighthouse at Alexandria was especially valuable to sailors. The lighthouse could be seen so far out to sea, that sailors could sail far from the coast and avoid shallow, underwater hazards while remaining in visual contact with the lighthouse.

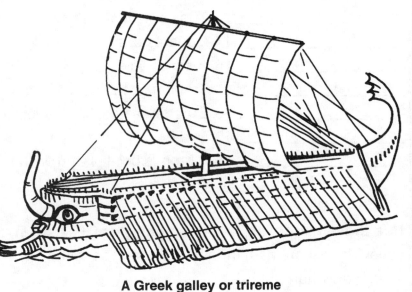

**A Greek galley or trireme**

Name _____ Date _____

# Sailing and Trading in Greece

Much of the vocabulary used to describe sailing and trading in ancient Greece is still used today. How well do you understand the following terms dealing with sailing and trading? Some of the terms were associated with ancient Greece and some are more modern. Below and to the right are a number of definitions. In the blank before each definition, write the word that is described by the definition. Choose from the terms given below.

**TERM**                                          **DEFINITION**

_____ 1. A hinged plate mounted at the stern of a vessel used to guide the ship.

_____ 2. Located at or toward the stern or rear of a ship.

_____ 3. Located at or toward the front of a ship.

_____ 4. To transport someone or something across a body of water by boat.

_____ 5. A pier or landing spot where ships load or unload.

_____ 6. Some type of barrier designed to protect a harbor from the full force of the waves.

_____ 7. The goods carried by a ship.

_____ 8. A large ship propelled by sails and oars used as a warship. Today the term also means the ship's kitchen.

_____ 9. A person who illegally brings goods into the country.

_____ 10. A person who works on a dock and loads and unloads ships.

_____ 11. A person hired to carry goods.

_____ 12. Merchants who made a living by exchanging one kind of currency for another.

_____ 13. A naval officer in charge of a ship's crew. In Greece, they used a flute to create a rhythm for the slaves to oar by.

_____ 14. The captain of a ship.

_____ 15. Capable of sailing.

_____ 16. A cargo ship.

_____ 17. Trading goods or services without exchanging money.

_____ 18. Broad-beamed, clumsy-looking ship designed to carry heavy cargo.

_____ 19. The bow or forward part of a ship's hull.

_____ 20. A bronze point placed on the prow of the ship used to ram into enemy ships.

**Use these words:** aft, barter, battering ram, boatswain, breakwater, cargo, ferry, fore, freighter, galley, longshoreman, money-changers, porter, prow, 'round ship', rudder, seaworthy, skipper, smuggler, wharf

# Archaeology and the Wonders of the World

Scientists tell us that humans have been living on earth for more than a million years. Who these people were, where they lived, and what their lives were like remain, for the most part, mysteries. Since writing was only invented a few thousand years ago, there is no record of the lives, cultures, and civilizations of the many people who lived before writing was invented. To understand these people, we can only study clues they have left behind. The clues are objects and other items that we are able to discover as we search where they lived. People who try to learn more about ancient cultures by studying clues are called **archaeologists**. The science of learning about ancient people is called **archaeology**. Archaeologists try to figure out where ancient people lived, and then they slowly and carefully **excavate** the area in order to find **artifacts** and **relics** that will reveal how these ancient people lived. For example, if they find spears, they might conclude the people who lived at this location were hunters or warriors. If they find tools used for farming or fishing, they will have an idea of the type of diet the people had. Sometimes archeologists even dive under the ocean to find relics from sunken ships or from costal areas where ancient cities have been flooded.

Compared to other sciences, archaeology is relatively new. Prior to the eighteenth century, little interest was taken in the distant past. Most people spent waking hours hunting, farming, or working, so little time was available for looking for artifacts. Of course, if someone found a relic that was made of precious metal or gems, the valuable ingredient was extracted and the rest of the relic was either discarded or destroyed.

One of the first great archaeological finds occurred in Italy in 1748. The remains of Pompeii, a Roman city that was destroyed and covered by ash and lava from the volcano Vesuvius, was discovered. Pompeii was destroyed in A.D. 79, and the volcano erupted so violently and quickly that people and animals were unable to escape. Consequently, the people and the city in which they lived were captured and, in a sense, frozen in time, enabling future generations to study this civilization.

When archaeologists find a **site** they think may have been inhabited by a civilization, they begin by sinking **trial shafts** to see if there is evidence that ancient humans lived or worked in the area. The shafts will also tell them how far down they need to dig in order to find what they are looking for. Next, they dig **trial trenches** to determine how far and wide the site is. Then the real digging begins.

Archaeologists use tools such as picks, trowels, knives, and brushes to carefully remove the earth and find artifacts. Once an item is removed, it is photographed, cataloged, and carefully stored for further tests. One of the things archeologists want to learn is how old the item is. Sometimes they can decide this by what the item is, the material it is made from, or how it is made. At other times, they use a method called **carbon dating**. Anything that once lived will release carbon slowly over several thousand years. By measuring the amount of carbon the item has left, archaeologists can determine its age.

Name _____ Date _____

# Archaeology Quiz

Here are some of the terms used in the field of archaeology. See if you can match the definitions with the words given below.

TERM                                           DEFINITION

_____ 1. A building where works of art or historical items are displayed for the public.

_____ 2. Digging for artifacts.

_____ 3. The years after the birth of Christ.

_____ 4. A method used to determine the age of some living thing that has died.

_____ 5. A trip for scientific study.

_____ 6. The years before Christ was born.

_____ 7. Cuts made in the earth to determine the size of an archaeological site.

_____ 8. An item from the past.

_____ 9. Holes dug to determine how far down a site exists.

_____ 10. A small shovel archaeologists use to dig.

_____ 11. A scientist who studies old civilizations and objects.

_____ 12. The science of studying old items.

_____ 13. An old item that was made by people of long ago.

_____ 14. Location where the dig is taking place.

_____ 15. Belonging to a period a long time ago.

_____ 16. To list and record.

_____ 17. The culture and society developed by a group of people.

_____ 18. The behavior patterns, beliefs, arts, and all other products of a particular group of people.

_____ 19. To convert the words of one language into the words of another.

_____ 20. Written materials.

**Use these words:** A.D., B.C., archaeologist, archaeology, artifact, ancient, carbon dating, catalog, civilization, culture, excavating, expedition, manuscripts, museum, relic, site, trial shafts, trial trenches, translate, trowel

54

# Other Wonders of the World
# Stonehenge

One of the reasons the Great Pyramid of Giza was classified as one of the Seven Wonders of the Ancient World was the fact that enormous stones were quarried, transported to the building site, and hoisted into place without the use of modern machines. This tremendous feat not only required great muscle power, but engineering skills as well.

What the Greek writer Antipater, who compiled the list of the Seven Wonders of the Ancient World, did not know, however, was that others were building monuments and structures with huge stones in other parts of the world. These large stones are sometimes referred to as **megaliths** and are used in **prehistoric** monuments or structures. One example is **Stonehenge** in southern England. A **henge** is a stone circle built by men in the Neolithic period. Construction may have begun on it almost 300 years before the Great Pyramid was built.

Actually, Stonehenge was built in three phases. The first phase was begun around 2800 B.C. and consisted of a platform encircled by a ditch and a bank. Over the next 1,500 years, many additions were made until there were two circles of 30 huge stones, measuring almost 14 feet high, placed on end. At the top of each pair of these stones rested a horizontal stone called a **lintel**. The lintels were placed with such precision that their ends touched, forming one enormous circle. This circle, in turn, enclosed five **trilithons**, two upright stones with one lintel across the top of them.

Stonehenge remains a mystery. Three questions remain unanswered—"How?", "Who?", and "Why?". How were the huge stones transported by these primitive people? Most of the stones came from a **quarry** about 20 miles from the construction site, but others may have come from the Prescelly Mountains in Wales over 100 miles away. The **bluestones** that make up the inner circle of Stonehenge weighed as much as four tons each, and about 80 stones were used in construction. They are called bluestones because they turn blue whenever they become wet. Considering these stones were moved in about 2000 B.C., about the same time that the pyramids were being built, this was quite an accomplishment. The huge **sarsen** stones form the outer ring of Stonehenge and weigh as much as 50 tons each. How were these huge stones moved? They were probably moved by a method similar to the one used by the Egyptians to build the pyramids. The stones were moved on rollers made of logs, pulled on **sledges,** and floated on barges.

We really don't know who built Stonehenge. It was probably begun in the late **Neolithic** period around 3000 B.C. and built in stages over a period of centuries. Many different cultures may have been involved in the construction. There is the persistent theory that the **Druids** constructed Stonehenge. This idea has been expressed by many writers throughout the years, but it is probably not true. The Druids, which were an order of Celtic priests, existed about 2,000 years after Stonehenge was constructed. History also shows that the Druids worshipped in forest temples, and it is not likely they would have worshipped in a stone temple.

What was the purpose of Stonehenge? Was it a ceremonial site or a religious temple? A popular notion is that Stonehenge was an astronomical observatory and was used by prehistoric humans as a calendar. While this can't be proven because Stonehenge is no longer intact, it is known that prehistoric people worshiped the Sun and that Stonehenge's **axis** points in the direction of the sunrise at the summer **solstice**. In any case, Stonehenge was an exceptional achievement of architecture, engineering, and astronomy.

Name _____ Date _____

# Stonehenge Vocabulary

How well do you understand the following terms dealing with Stonehenge? Below and to the right are a number of definitions. In the blank before each definition, write the word that is described by the definition. Choose from the terms given below.

**TERM**

**DEFINITION**

_____  1. A large, flat-bottomed boat used for transporting freight.

_____  2. A structure, such as a stone sculpture, constructed as a memorial.

_____  3. A large stone used in various prehistoric construction.

_____  4. A pit from which stone is obtained by digging and cutting. Today, the stone may be blasted to remove it.

_____  5. A circle of standing stones on Salisbury Plain in England built by prehistoric people.

_____  6. The stones from which the first inner circle was built. The stones were thought to be from the Prescelly Mountains.

_____  7. A device mounted on runners used to transport heavy objects. People in the United States use the term "sled."

_____  8. A horizontal beam that forms the upper part of a window, door, or other structure.

_____  9. The study of the positions, dimensions, motion, and evolution of celestial bodies.

_____  10. Before recorded history.

_____  11. The period around 10,000 B.C. that is distinguished by the development of agriculture and the making of polished stone implements.

_____  12. An area or building designed and arranged to view and study the sky, the stars, and other celestial bodies.

_____  13. A line of reference from which distances or angles are measured.

_____  14. The giant stones that form the outer circle, which weigh as much as 50 tons each.

_____  15. An order of Celtic priests.

_____  16. Two upright stones with one lintel across the top of them.

_____  17. A circle of stones.

**Use these words:** astronomical observatory, astronomy, axis, barge, bluestones, Druids, henge, lintel, megaliths, monument, Neolithic, prehistoric, quarry, sarsen, sledge, Stonehenge, trilithons

# The Great Wall of China

Another wonder omitted from the list of the Seven Wonders of the Ancient World was the **Great Wall of China**. Actually the Wall is not a single wall built of stone, but two walls that average about ten feet apart and run parallel to each other. The area between the walls was filled with earth and then lined with stone, forming a road. At intervals along the walls are **watchtowers** rising above the wall. These watchtowers were places where **sentries** were stationed to watch for invaders.

Like the ancient pyramids and Stonehenge, creation of the Great Wall of China involved the moving of many massive stones in order to fashion this marvelous structure. In the case of China's wall, however, it is not the size or weight of the stones that is impressive; it is the length of the wall that is remarkable. The wall, which ran along the border between China and enemy territories in the north, is about 30 feet high and 1,500 miles long . To have a better understanding of how long 1,500 miles is, picture a wall that begins in New York City and ends in Oklahoma City. Or imagine a wall that begins in Boston, Massachusetts, and extends to Omaha, Nebraska. Or one that reaches from Toronto, Ontario, Canada, all the way to Miami, Florida. Each of these walls would be a few miles *shorter* than the Great Wall of China.

One of the great mysteries is: *How long was the original wall?* That is hard to determine since the Great Wall was not a single wall but many separate walls built over 2,000 years. The wall began as an earthen wall supported by planks. It was built in segments by different states and was only a few miles long. In about 221 B.C., **Ch'in Shih Huang Ti**, the first Ch'in emperor of China, drafted peasants and forced slaves to link these walls into one long wall and to make it more formidable in order to discourage invaders. After the **Ch'in Dynasty**, other dynasties increased the length, expanding and enlarging the wall until it was finished in about 204 B.C. Even after the wall was completed, the Chinese continued working on it, making it more elaborate and modern in design. The stone wall, as we know it today, began during the **Ming Dynasty**, which lasted from 1368 to 1644. The remaining sections of the wall were built during this time. The wall built during the Ming Dynasty was strong, over 4,500 miles long, and was patrolled by 100,000 soldiers. At points where the leaders thought invaders were likely to attack, as many as nine walls were built parallel to each other. Eventually cannons were added, making the Wall even more secure.

For many centuries, armies were stationed along the Wall to provide a warning of advancing invaders. The soldiers would signal their countrymen by building fires in the towers at the first sign of an enemy. The Wall enabled the army to provide an excellent defense until reinforcements arrived. Since the Wall was so high, the invaders were forced to scale the walls as the defenders used spears and arrows on the advancing enemy. Consequently, the Chinese army could defend against a larger number of invaders because of the strategic advantage provided by the Wall.

Unfortunately, the entire length of the wall does not exist today. It suffers from the same fate as the pyramids and other great structures of the past. Parts of the Wall have been taken down and used to build other structures. However, when the Great Wall was intact, it was surely one of mankind's greatest achievements. Even today, it remains the largest structure ever created by humans.

Name _____ Date _____

# Great Wall of China Synonyms

Shown below are several words used in the description of the Great Wall of China. Look at each word written in bold-face type and then find the word at the right that has *almost* the same meaning. Words that have the same meaning are called synonyms. Write the synonym in the blank in front of the word in bold-face type. Then write a sentence using that synonym on the line below each group of words.

_____ 1. **parallel**      A. collateral       B. key           C. tall

_____ 2. **sentries**      A. priests          B. guards        C. farmers

_____ 3. **intervals**     A. crests           B. blocks        C. spaces

_____ 4. **peasants**      A. birds            B. farmers       C. soldiers

_____ 5. **formidable**    A. attractive       B. difficult     C. colorful

_____ 6. **dynasty**       A. reign            B. cooks         C. celebrities

_____ 7. **elaborate**     A. simple           B. drab          C. intricate

_____ 8. **strategic**     A. vital            B. curious       C. luxurious

_____ 9. **stationed**     A. posted           B. pumped        C. released

_____ 10. **massive**      A. minute           B. huge          C. average

_____ 11. **fashion**      A. decorate         B. paint         C. construct

_____ 12. **segments**     A. sections         B. connections   C. catacombs

_____ 13. **link**         A. separate         B. join          C. divide

_____ 14. **drafted**      A. hired            B. asked         C. inducted

_____ 15. **omitted**      A. overlooked       B. included      C. added

# The Colosseum of Rome

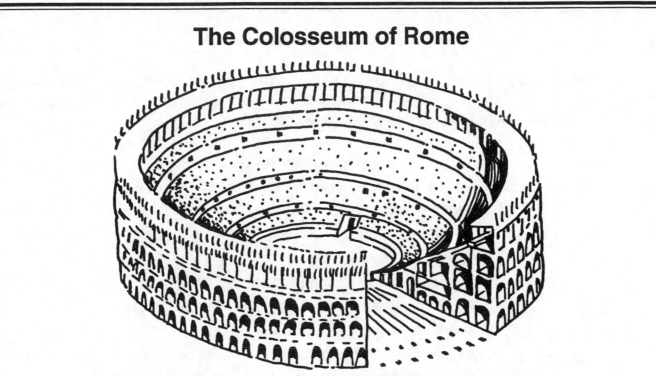

**This diagram shows a cutaway view of the interior of the Colosseum.**

Almost every Roman city had an open air **stadium** where public games and shows were held. The largest stadium was in Rome and was called the **Colosseum**. The massive structure was so impressive that an eighth century historian named Bede said, "As long as the Colosseum stands, Rome shall stand; when the Colosseum falls, Rome shall fall; when Rome falls, the world shall end."

The Colosseum was built between the Esquiline and Palatine hills, near the **Forum**. It was named Colosseum because it was built next to a colossal statue of Nero, a Roman emperor. Construction of the Colosseum was begun by Vespasian and completed by his son, Titus, in A.D. 81. The huge **elliptical** structure is 160 feet high, 620 feet long, and 510 feet wide. It is one third of a mile in length, covers over six acres, and is four stories high with **ramped** seating that could accommodate about 50,000 spectators.

Inside the Colosseum is a four-tiered **gallery** with **arcades** on the first three levels. The **arches** in the arcades have attached three-quarter columns. The styles of the columns are different. **Doric** columns are on the first level. **Ionic** columns are on the second, and **Corinthian** columns adorn the third level. The top story of the structure has Corinthian **pilasters**. The **amphitheater** was so well designed, with over 80 entrances, that all of the spectators could evacuate the structure in a matter of minutes.

Beneath the arena floor is a **substructure,** almost 40 feet deep, which consists of a system of **corridors**. These corridors were originally designed to keep slaves and animals who were used for the "games" that took place in the Colosseum. The area beneath the arena floor also had plumbing that was used to fill the floor with water for mock sea battles.

Although admission to the Colosseum was free, the seating was assigned according to social standing. The first **tier** was reserved for the emperor, his family, and court. **Aristocrats** sat in the second tier, while women were required to sit in the third tier. The top level was for the common people.

The Colosseum represents, to a great degree, the best in Roman architecture. Its construction techniques and engineering make the Colosseum an impressive structure.

Name _____ Date _____

# Colosseum Vocabulary

How well do you understand the following terms dealing with the Colosseum? Below and to the right are a number of definitions. In the blank before each definition, write the word that is described by the definition. Choose from the terms given below.

**TERM**                          **DEFINITION**

_____ 1. One of a number of rows placed one above another.

_____ 2. A form of architecture in Greece known for its simplicity and austerity.

_____ 3. An oval or a round arena that has tiers of seats that rise gradually outward from the center.

_____ 4. An amphitheater built in Rome in A.D. 81.

_____ 5. A form of Greek architecture that is very elaborate.

_____ 6. The foundation or area below a structure.

_____ 7. A type of Greek architecture known for its grace and elegance. The top of a column might appear to be a pair of ram's horns.

_____ 8. A series of arches supported by columns.

_____ 9. A rectangular column that has been set into a wall as a decorative element.

_____ 10. A narrow hallway or passageway. In some cases rooms open off of it.

_____ 11. An architectural structure that forms a curved, pointed, or flat upper edge of an open space and supports the weight above.

_____ 12. An inclined surface that connects different levels.

_____ 13. A group of people considered superior—nobility.

_____ 14. The public square or marketplace in an ancient Roman city where public business was transacted.

_____ 15. A narrow balcony.

_____ 16. Shaped like an oval.

_____ 17. The Colosseum could be flooded for these.

_____ 18. Roman emperor who began construction of the Colosseum.

_____ 19. Those who sat in the top level.

_____ 20. The first tier was reserved for this person and his court.

**Use these words:** amphitheater, arcade, arch, aristocracy, Colosseum, common people, Corinthian, corridor, Doric, elliptical, emperor, forum, gallery, Ionic, pilaster, ramp, sea battles, substructure, tier, Vespasian

60

# The Roman Games

Traces of the ancient Roman Empire are still with us today. Our system of government, language, law, architecture, art, religion, and our calendar were all influenced by this ancient culture. There is one legacy, however, we have not adopted. It is the savage cruelty of their "entertainment," which was held in an outdoor stadium.

The entertainment in ancient Rome consisted of public games and shows held on holidays. The games were all-day affairs that included a wide variety of activities, such as gladiatorial contests. Gladiatorial fights were armed fights between two men, which may have originated as a funeral activity to honor the deceased, but became so popular they were made part of the games at the amphitheater.

Gladiators were slaves, prisoners of war, or criminals who trained to fight in special ways, and eventually they were forced to fight to their death before spectators. The types of fights varied, but the one that was the most popular and has been portrayed in movies, such as *Spartacus*, occurred between two gladiators. One did not have any armor, but looked like a fisherman. He carried a three-pronged spear and a net. His opponent was fully armed. The object was for the one with the net to entangle his opponent and throw him to the ground, while the one in full armor tried to get the other at his mercy. When one was clearly the winner, he looked at the audience. If the crowd wanted the loser to live, they would put their thumbs up. If they wanted him killed, their thumbs would be put down.

In addition to gladiatorial contests, the ampitheater often featured hunts of wild or exotic animals. Trees would be planted in the arena and wild animals such as tigers, antelope, polar bears, and rhinoceroses would be turned loose for hunters to kill. There were times, of course, when the hunters were unsuccessful, and they were attacked and killed by the animals. Another activity you may have seen in the movies involved unarmed humans and wild animals. Sometimes criminals, slaves, Christians, or other oppressed groups of people were placed in the arena with hungry lions, tigers, or bears to be slaughtered for the entertainment of the Roman spectators.

Not all of the events were as cruel as the ones just described. Perhaps the most popular event was the chariot race. You may have seen an example of this type of entertainment in the movie *Ben Hur*. The races featured twelve chariots that made seven laps around the arena. Each race was about five miles long. Collisions were common as the racers turned the corners. The Circus Maximus in Rome, a 700-yard-long oval stadium that could hold about 150,000 people, was the most famous arena for chariot races.

Another spectacular event was the mock sea battle held in an arena. The arena would be flooded, and war ships would be brought in. The contestants would fight just as though it were a real battle. On the surface this might appear to be a "pretend" war, but every effort was made to make it appear real. People were actually killed in these mock battles.

Name _____ Date _____

# Create a Roman Character

Listed below are some of the people who lived and were involved in the Roman Games. In the blanks below each person's name, write a brief description of what you think that person might have been like. The description should not only include what they looked like, but it should also tell us as much about their personality and habits as possible.

Emperor _____

_____

_____

_____

Aristocrat _____

_____

_____

_____

Slave _____

_____

_____

_____

Gladiator _____

_____

_____

_____

Christian _____

_____

_____

_____

Soldier _____

_____

_____

_____

Craftsman or Builder _____

_____

_____

_____

Name _____ Date _____

Choose one of the people you have just described. Give him a name and answer the following questions about him. However, instead of using the description and characteristics that you used to describe him before, *make the character exactly opposite of the one you described.* In other words, if you said the character was cruel, he would now become kind.

Person: _____

Name: _____

Write a brief physical description: _____

_____

_____

What is this person like? _____

_____

_____

_____

List any habits of speech or gestures: _____

_____

_____

_____

Tell about his personal life—family, parents, spouse, children, etc. _____

_____

_____

_____

Use this information to write his account of a day at the Colosseum from his point of view. Use a lot of description. What is the weather like? Who can he see or hear? What is he thinking? What is he feeling? Use the back of the sheet to complete your story.

_____

_____

_____

_____

_____

_____

_____

_____

_____

_____

_____

Name _____ Date _____

# Terms in Ancient Roman Life Crossword Puzzle

There are many terms used today that either had their beginnings in ancient Rome or were an important part of Roman society. See if you can figure out what they were. Use the clues below to complete the crossword puzzle.

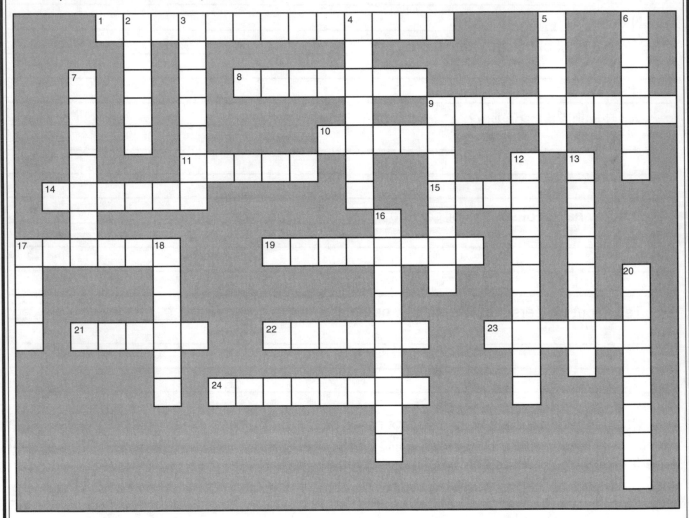

**ACROSS**

1. A political murder
8. A common person in Rome
9. A fighter whose fights were considered a public sport
10. A painting that covers a wall or ceiling
11. A group of barbarians
14. A written agreement between nations
15. A loose garment
17. The ruling council of ancient Rome
19. A ruler with absolute authority
21. Term for a war between groups within the same country
22. Art created by using inlaid pieces of glass or stone
23. In ancient Rome, an arena for sports events
24. Form of government in which citizens elect representatives to govern them

**DOWN**

2. A long attack
3. Chaos due to lack of government
4. A Roman official who protected the common people from laws
5. A Roman garment that slipped over the head and was belted at the waist
6. A territory that belongs to a country
7. A soldier who has served for a long period
9. One who overeats
12. A three-dimensional sculpture on a flat background
13. A channel that water flows through
16. A Roman noble
17. To take the valuables from those who were defeated
18. A government that covers a large area
20. A court of justice and a style of Catholic Church common in Rome

# The Taj Mahal

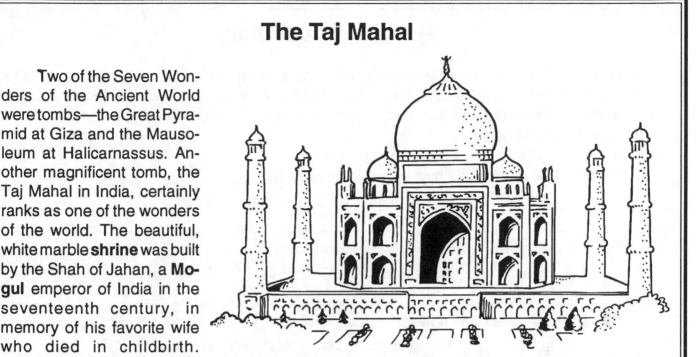

Two of the Seven Wonders of the Ancient World were tombs—the Great Pyramid at Giza and the Mausoleum at Halicarnassus. Another magnificent tomb, the Taj Mahal in India, certainly ranks as one of the wonders of the world. The beautiful, white marble **shrine** was built by the Shah of Jahan, a **Mogul** emperor of India in the seventeenth century, in memory of his favorite wife who died in childbirth. Mumtaz-i-Mahal was not only married to the **Shah**, she was his friend, counselor, and advisor. They were inseparable. She accompanied him on all of his journeys and was beloved by everyone because of her concern for the people the Shah ruled. She bore the Shah 14 children in 19 years and died in 1630. In his grief, the Shah decided to build his wife a tomb magnificent enough to match his love for her. It took 22 years and the labor of over 20,000 workers to complete the tomb and the surrounding complex.

The Shah planned to construct a **replica** of the Taj out of black marble on the other side of the Jumna River for his tomb, but before he could begin, his son seized the throne and imprisoned his father. Eventually, the Shah died and was buried in the Taj near his wife.

The Taj is considered to be one of the most splendid buildings in the world. It is known not only for its unequalled beauty, but also for its elegant design. The unusual **aura** of light as the sunlight reflects off the white marble **facade** of the tomb and the red sandstone of the surrounding buildings gives the viewer a dreamlike view of the structure.

What many people do not know is that the tomb is not an **isolated** memorial, but part of a **complex** that also includes a main gateway, garden, **mosque**, and prayer house. The architecture of the Taj represents the style of mausoleums that originated in Iran and Central Asia and developed in India. This type of architecture uses elements such as the white, onion-shaped, double-dome top, a high **portal**, and corner **domes**.

The tomb itself is square with **chamfered** corners, and it is about 187 feet tall. It stands on a marble **plinth**, which rests on a red **sandstone** platform. Four tall **minarets,** or towers, arise from the corners of the white marble plinth. The doorways are decorated with **calligraphy**.

Part of the beauty of the Taj is the garden that runs from the main gateway to the Taj. At the center of the garden, halfway between the tomb and the gateway, stands a raised marble **lotus-**tank that was placed to **mirror** the Taj in the water.

The tomb was originally inlaid with many precious stones, such as **diamonds**, **sapphires**, and **jade**. A solid gold barrier was erected around the coffin of Mumtaz. Pearls and diamonds were also placed around Mumtaz's coffin. Soldiers guarded the tomb to protect it from robbers. Eventually the Mogul empire fell, and the tomb was **looted**, but it was not destroyed.

Name _____ Date _____

# Taj Mahal Vocabulary

Read each of the following sentences that have been adapted from the information on the Taj Mahal. Below each sentence are four words. One of these words is a synonym for the word that is in bold print. Circle the word that *most nearly matches,* and write a sentence of your own that uses the word in bold type.

1. The beautiful **shrine** was built by the Shah of Jahan.
   A. sanctuary       B. alabaster       C. luminous       D. altar

_____

2. The Shah of Jahan was a **Mogul** emperor of India.
   A. cruel          B. handsome        C. famous         D. Mongol

_____

3. The **Shah** of Jahan was a Mogul emperor of India in the seventeenth century.
   A. hero           B. monarch         C. celebrity      D. peasant

_____

4. The Shah planned to construct a black marble **replica** of the Taj for his tomb.
   A. mausoleum  B. shrine            C. copy           D. monument

_____

5. The Shah's son **seized** the throne and imprisoned his father.
   A. observed       B. inherited       C. accepted       D. grabbed

_____

6. Dusk provides an unusual **aura** of light as the sunlight reflects off the white marble.
   A. location       B. quiet           C. intensity      D. atmosphere

_____

7. The sunlight reflects off the white marble **facade** of the tomb.
   A. veneer         B. color           C. stone          D. top

_____

8. What many people do not know is that the tomb is not an **isolated** memorial.
   A. painted        B. new             C. solitary       D. atrocious

_____

9. The tomb is part of a **complex.**
   A. city           B. group           C. cemetery       D. catacomb

_____

10. The complex also includes a main gateway, garden, **mosque,** and prayer house.
    A. gift shop      B. solarium        C. orchard        D. church

_____

66

Name _____ Date _____

11. This type of architecture uses elements such as a high **portal**.

    A. porthole     B. entrance     C. window     D. dome

12. This type of architecture uses elements such as a high **dome**.

    A. round window  B. entrance     C. portal     D. hemispherical roof

13. The tomb itself is square with **chamfered** corners.

    A. beveled     B. square     C. round     D. oval

14. The tomb stands on a marble **plinth**.

    A. column     B. base     C. roof     D. statue

15. Four tall **minarets** arise from the corners of the white marble plinth.

    A. towers     B. balconies     C. columns     D. poles

16. The doorways are decorated with **calligraphy**.

    A. stencils     B. wallpaper     C. handwriting   D. decorations

17. At the center of the garden is a raised marble **lotus**-tank.

    A. plant     B. fish     C. insect     D. pretty

18. The tomb was inlaid with many precious stones such as diamonds and **sapphires.**

    A. prizes     B. gems     C. gifts     D. treasures

19. Eventually the Mogul **empire** fell.

    A. tomb     B. minarets     C. dome     D. nation

20. Eventually the Mogul empire fell and the tomb was **looted**, but it was not destroyed.

    A. demolished  B. refurbished  C. painted     D. plundered

21. Many people do not know the tomb is not an isolated **memorial.**

    A. building     B. tomb     C. monument     D. attraction

22. A raised marble lotus-tank was placed to **mirror** the Taj in the water.

    A. show     B. reflect     C. reveal     D. hide

# The Statue of Liberty

The Statue of Liberty might well be called the Colossus of the United States. It is similar in size, appearance, and construction to the Colossus of Rhodes, and both were built near a harbor. Their effect on visitors was also similar. Travelers sailing into the harbor to Rhodes were struck by the size, beauty, and engineering achievement of the Colossus. They were also in awe because the statue represented a god. Travelers sailing into the New York harbor are also struck by the size, beauty, and engineering achievement of the Statue of Liberty. However, this statue does not represent a god or a real person, but an idea or ideal. The Statue of Liberty is a symbol of hope, freedom, and liberty for millions of immigrants who have come to America to begin a new life.

While the Statue of Liberty is a symbol of the United States, it was not built or paid for by Americans. Originally called *Liberty Enlightening the World*, the Statue of Liberty was a gift from the French people to the United States in honor of the 1876 centennial celebration. The idea for the statue even began in France. Edouard-Rene Lefebvre de Laboulaye, a prominent teacher in France, loved America and the freedoms that its citizens were able to enjoy. He wrote several books about the United States. He was supposed to teach law in the College of France, but instead, he taught his students everything he knew about the United States. At a dinner party one evening, Laboulaye was talking about what a wonderful country the United States was and that France had helped the United States win their independence from Great Britain. He suggested that France and the United States, who were friends, should build a monument to freedom together and place it in the United States. Frédéric Auguste Bartholdi, who was a well-known sculptor, was at the party, became excited about the idea, and decided he would be the one to design and build the monument.

Bartholdi decided to visit the United States to become more acquainted with the country and the people. When his ship arrived in New York Harbor, he saw a little island called Bedloe's Island and decided that this was the spot for his monument—a statue. While in the United States, he talked to famous and common people and told them all his idea about a statue. He even spoke to President Ulysses S. Grant. His trip encouraged him to pursue the project. He returned to France and eventually began working on the project.

First, he designed the statue, which he called *Liberty Enlightening the World*. Bartholdi's mother served as a model for the face. In the statue's left arm is a tablet with the date of the Declaration of Independence written in Roman numerals. Her right arm is held high and has a torch lighting the way and welcoming immigrants and visitors. At the statues's feet is a broken chain that symbolizes how the United States broke free from Great Britain.

In order to fund the project, Laboulaye formed a French-American Union. Villages, businesses, and individuals all donated to build the statue. The committee even held a lottery with all of the proceeds going to construction of the statue. School children in France also collected money to build the statue. By the end of 1875, enough money had been raised to begin work.

Bartholdi had decided not to build the statue out of stone. He thought that a steel frame covered with copper would be better. Since the statue was going to be created in France, shipped to the United States, and then assembled, a framework construction seemed more practical. But who could he get to design the framework? He was an artist, not an engineer. Bartholdi hired an engineer named Alexandre Gustave Eiffel to design the support system. Eiffel had built many steel bridges and would become famous in the future for building a great tower in Paris. The Eiffel Tower is as famous as the Statue of Liberty and is considered by many to be a wonder of the modern world.

The statue was not completed in time for the 1876 centennial celebration, but the right hand with the torch was finished and put on display for the celebration. The head of the statue was also on display in 1878 for the World's Fair held in Paris. Even after the entire statue was completed, it could not be erected because the base on Bedloe's Island wasn't ready. Work had begun, but the workers ran out of money and Americans refused to donate any more for the project. The French had designed and built the statue, but the base and pedestal were the responsibility of the United States.

Joseph Pulitzer, who owned a newspaper called *The World,* was a Hungarian immigrant who took on the cause to fund the pedestal and base. He wrote about liberty and freedom. He criticized the rich for not contributing and encouraged even ordinary citizens to donate. He also published the names of everyone who contributed. Eventually, enough money was collected and the statue was erected and unveiled in New York Harbor on October 26, 1886.

Inscribed on the base of the statue is a famous poem written by Emma Lazarus.

### THE NEW COLOSSUS

Not like the brazen giant of Greek fame,
With conquering limbs astride from land to land;
Here at our sea-washed, sunset gates shall stand
A mighty woman with a torch, whose flame
Is the imprisoned lightning, and her name
Mother of Exiles. From her beacon-hand
Glows world-wide welcome; her mild eyes command
The air-bridged harbor that twin cities frame.
"Keep, ancient lands, your storied pomp!" cries she
With silent lips. "Give me your tired, your poor,
Your huddled masses yearning to breathe free,
The wretched refuse of your teeming shore.
Send these, the homeless, tempest-tost to me,
I lift my lamp beside the golden door!"

Name _____ Date _____

# Comparing the Statue of Liberty With the Colossus of Rhodes

Many people have compared the Statue of Liberty to the Colossus of Rhodes. How do you think they compare? On the left are facts concerning the Colossus of Rhodes. Fill in the corresponding facts concerning the Statue of Liberty.

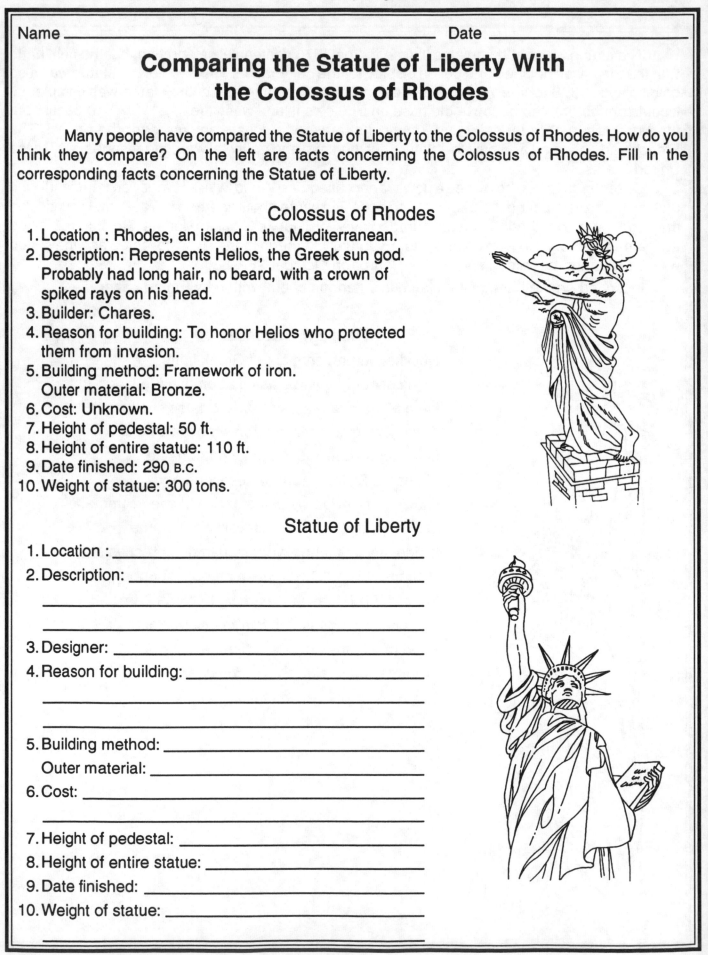

## Colossus of Rhodes

1. Location : Rhodes, an island in the Mediterranean.
2. Description: Represents Helios, the Greek sun god. Probably had long hair, no beard, with a crown of spiked rays on his head.
3. Builder: Chares.
4. Reason for building: To honor Helios who protected them from invasion.
5. Building method: Framework of iron. Outer material: Bronze.
6. Cost: Unknown.
7. Height of pedestal: 50 ft.
8. Height of entire statue: 110 ft.
9. Date finished: 290 B.C.
10. Weight of statue: 300 tons.

## Statue of Liberty

1. Location : _____
2. Description: _____
   _____
   _____
3. Designer: _____
4. Reason for building: _____
   _____
   _____
5. Building method: _____
   Outer material: _____
6. Cost: _____
   _____
7. Height of pedestal: _____
8. Height of entire statue: _____
9. Date finished: _____
10. Weight of statue: _____
    _____

Name _____ Date _____

# Rewriting the Statue of Liberty Inscription

You have read the poem by Emma Lazarus that appears on the base of the Statue of Liberty. Do you think it is appropriate today? Could it be improved?

Your assignment is to write a new inscription for the base of the Statue of Liberty you think would be more appropriate or better than the one that appears now. It can convey the same message that the present inscription conveys or, it might be completely different. Your inscription may be a poem, but it does *not* have to rhyme.

# Statues

The artistic endeavors of humans have always been inspiring. Among the Seven Wonders of the Ancient World, two are statues. They are the Statue of Zeus at Olympus and the Colossus of Rhodes. Other impressive statues have been created over the years that many feel are just as impressive as these two. Four are listed below.

## THE GREAT SPHINX

The sphinx is a legendary creature, which combined the body of a lion and the head of a man in a crouching position. The sphinx is a popular subject for ancient Egyptian sculpture, and statues of sphinxes were often placed in pyramids. By far, the most famous sphinx is found near the Great Pyramid of Giza, one of the Seven Wonders of the Ancient World. Named the Great Sphinx, the Sphinx of Giza measures 240 feet long and 66 feet high and is probably around 4,500 years old. Originally built to guard the Great Pyramid, the Great Sphinx is one of Egypt's most famous monuments. There is speculation that the face of the Great Sphinx was that of Kharafe, the king at the time the Sphinx was built.

## EASTER ISLAND

Easter Island in the South Pacific is over 2,000 miles from the nearest population center. In spite of the fact that it is one of the most isolated places on Earth, the island has been a source of curiosity and mystery for archaeologists and scientists for many years. The source of this curiosity is the 600 huge statues carved out of volcanic rock that have been placed at various locations around this island. While most are between 10 and 20 feet high, the largest one is 37 feet. Some of the statues weigh up to 50 U.S. tons. What makes these immense statues a puzzle is, "Who carved them and why?"

Archaeologists are still unsure how the first people came to Easter Island, since it is more than 2,000 miles from South America and 1,200 miles to the nearest neighboring island. Most scientists feel the residents of Easter Island came from other South Pacific islands, although some feel they could have traveled all the way from South America. Wherever they came from, they apparently arrived around A.D. 400 and began carving the statues, which are known as Moai. The statues were carved with stone tools and apparently transported from quarries within the volcano of Rano Raruku.

## MOUNT RUSHMORE

The Black Hills of South Dakota are home to one of the most amazing sculptures of modern times. Carved into the granite cliffs of Mount Rushmore are the faces of four American presidents—George Washington, Thomas Jefferson, Theodore Roosevelt, and Abraham Lincoln. The sculptures are 60 feet high and took over 14 years to complete.

The original idea for a sculpture came from Doane Robinson, an historian associated with the South Dakota Historical Society. His idea, however, was not to have statues of presidents carved, but to have heroes of the west immortalized in stone. Gutzon Borglum, a well-known sculptor, was hired to do the job. The actual carving, which for the most part, was done by using dynamite, began in 1927. Today, over 2.5 million tourists visit Mount Rushmore National Park each year.

## THE CORCOVADO CHRIST

If you have ever seen a movie or a news story that takes place in Rio de Janeiro, Brazil, it is likely you have seen one of the most impressive statues in this hemisphere. The Corcovado Christ is a 130-foot-high concrete statue that is set on Mount Corcovado. The visitor who arrives by plane is welcomed by this magnificent statue of Christ, who is shown with outstretched arms.

Name _____ Date _____

# Research on Statues

Shown below are a number of questions. In order to find the answers, you need to do research in the library. First answer the question, and then list what resource you used in order to find the answer.

1. Question: Of what material was the Great Sphinx made?

   Answer: _____

   Source: _____

2. Question: Some think that the Sphinx is the embodiment of Harmakhis. Who was that?

   Answer: _____

   Source: _____

3. Question: Who was buried in the Great Pyramid of Giza?

   Answer: _____

   Source: _____

4. Question: Legend says in a dream, Prince Thutmose IV was ordered to clear the sand away

   from the Sphinx. What did he receive in return?

   Answer: _____

   Source: _____

5. Question: Which European discovered Easter Island? When?

   Answer: _____

   Source: _____

6. Question: What was his nationality?

   Answer: _____

   Source: _____

7. Question: Why did he name it Easter Island?

   Answer: _____

   Source: _____

Name _____ Date _____

8. Question: To which country does Easter Island belong?

   Answer: _____

   Source: _____

9. Question: Who decided which presidents should be carved on Mount Rushmore?

   Answer: _____

   Source: _____

10. Question: For what other sculptures was Borglum known?

    Answer: _____

    _____

    _____

    Source: _____

11. Question: Which president's head was carved first on Mount Rushmore?

    Answer: _____

    Source: _____

12. Question: Which president's head on Mt. Rushmore needed to be demolished because the

    stone was not sound?

    Answer: _____

    Source: _____

13. Question: What was the most serious health problem workers on Rushmore dealt with?

    Answer: _____

    Source: _____

14. Question: Who was the sculptor that created the Corcovado Christ?

    Answer: _____

    Source: _____

15. Question: How long did the Corcovado Christ take to complete, and when was it completed?

    Answer: _____

    Source: _____

Name _____ Date _____

# Identifying Well-Known Statues

Many magnificent statues have been created over the years. Some have been considered "wonders of the world," while others are just memorable works of art that represent the artistic accomplishments of humans. Can you identify the statues shown below? Choose from the statues listed below.

|  | NAME | LOCATION |
|---|---|---|
| 1.  | _____ | _____ |
| 2.  | _____ | _____ |
| 3.  | _____ | _____ |
| 4.  | _____ | _____ |
| 5.  | _____ | _____ |
| 6.  | _____ | _____ |
| 7.  | _____ | _____ |
| 8.  | _____ | _____ |

**Use these names:** Corcovado Christ, Great Sphinx, Easter Island Statues, Mount Rushmore Sculptures, Iwo Jima Memorial, Lincoln from his memorial, Stone Mountain, Statue of Liberty

Name _____ Date _____

# Buildings, Temples, and Monuments

The desire to build elaborate structures such as temples or monuments is almost as old as humankind. The artistic endeavors of humans have always been inspiring. Among the Seven Wonders of the Ancient world, five would be placed in this category. They are the Great Pyramid at Giza, the Hanging Gardens of Babylon, the Temple of Artemis at Ephesus, the Mausoleum of Mausolus at Halicarnassus, and the Lighthouse at Alexandria. Other outstanding structures have been created over the years that many feel are just as impressive as these Ancient Wonders. Shown below are pictures of some of these structures. Opposite each picture, you are to write the name of the structure and where it is located. Choose from the structures listed on the next page.

| | NAME | LOCATION |
|---|---|---|
| 1. | _____ | _____ |
| 2. | _____ | _____ |
| 3. | _____ | _____ |
| 4. | _____ | _____ |
| 5. | _____ | _____ |
| 6. | _____ | _____ |
| 7. | _____ | _____ |
| 8. | _____ | _____ |

Name 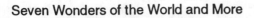 Date _____

|  | NAME | LOCATION |
|---|---|---|
| 9. | _____ | _____ |
| 10. | _____ | _____ |
| 11. | _____ | _____ |
| 12. | _____ | _____ |
| 13. | _____ | _____ |
| 14. | _____ | _____ |
| 15. | _____ | _____ |
| 16. | _____ | _____ |
| 17. | _____ | _____ |
| 18. | _____ | _____ |

**Use these words:** Arc de Triomphe, Big Ben, Colosseum, Eiffel Tower, Golden Gate Bridge, Gateway Arch, Great Wall of China, Leaning Tower of Pisa, Lincoln Memorial, Parthenon, Pyramid, St. Basil's Cathedral, St. Paul's Cathedral, Space Needle, Stonehenge, Sydney Opera House, Taj Mahal, Washington Monument

Name _____ Date _____

# Overlooked Wonders

You have read the list of the wonders of the world. There are many other structures that some think should be included but were not. Here are some of them.

- The Colosseum of Rome
- The Leaning Tower of Pisa
- The Mosque of Hagia Sophia
- The Parthenon at Athens
- Angkor Wat in Cambodia
- The Inca city of Machu Picchu, Peru
- The Statues on Easter Island
- Petra, the rock-carved city in Jordan
- Stonehenge in England
- The Golden Gate Bridge in San Francisco
- Hoover Dam in Arizona/Nevada, USA

- The Great Wall of China
- The Porcelain Tower of Nanking
- Taj Mahal in Agra, India
- The Statue of Liberty at New York
- The Aztec Temple in Mexico
- The Mayan Temples of Guatemala
- The Palace of Persepolis in Iran
- Mount Rushmore in South Dakota, USA
- The Temple of the Inscriptions in Mexico
- The High Dam in Aswan, Egypt
- Itaipú Dam in Brazil/Paraguay

Choose one of these wonders to write a description of to include in a book entitled *The Wonders of the World*.

The wonder: _____

Conduct research on the wonder you have selected. Find out all you can about this topic. Get facts, statistics, data, dates, and quotations. Then, write your description on your own paper.

1. Open your description with a lead paragraph that will catch the reader's attention and encourage them to read the entire story.
2. Write the description or story of the structure. You might want to use a chronological method to organize your story.
3. End with a paragraph that summarizes the wonders of this structure.

# Natural Wonders of the World

The original list of the Seven Wonders of the World included only structures and art objects created by humans. The world has many other wonders that might be called "natural" wonders. These are wonders of nature. Magnificent waterfalls, huge mountains, and beautiful deserts, just to name a few. Below are the descriptions of some of the most amazing natural wonders of the world.

## ANGEL FALLS

High on a plateau in the rain forest in southeastern Venezuela is Angel Falls. Located in Canaima National Park, Angel Falls is the highest waterfall in the world. The longest uninterrupted drop of the falls is about 2,640 feet, before the water flows into the Caroni River. That drop is about 20 times the drop of Niagara Falls.

## GRAND CANYON

The Grand Canyon is the largest gorge in the world. Located in northwestern Arizona, the Canyon is a mile deep in some places and 18 miles across at its widest point. The Canyon was carved by the Colorado River, which still snakes its way around the canyon walls on its journey to the Gulf of California. Within Grand Canyon National Park, the Colorado River is 105 miles long.

The walls of the Canyon, composed of layers of sandstone, limestone, lava, and other materials, reveal a rich history of the earth and a wealth of information for scientists. It is the beauty of the Canyon, however, that is of interest to most people. The distinctive appearance of the Canyon is constantly changing as the time of day and the seasons change.

## THE GREAT BARRIER REEF

The Great Barrier Reef lies in the Coral Sea in the Pacific Ocean, off the coast of Queensland, Australia. The Great Barrier Reef is actually a series of coral islands and reefs that extends for 1,259 miles, making it the longest reef in the world.

The reef consists of living coral, as well as the calcified remains of coral. Coral is a group of invertebrate animals and is often identified by their skeletons. Accumulation of these skeletal remains of coral over millions of years have developed unusual and beautiful formations.

## IGUACU FALLS

Located on the Iguacu River, between Argentina and Brazil, is Iguacu Falls. The Falls have hundreds of cataracts, some of which fall almost 300 feet. The falls are so magnificent that both Argentina and Brazil have established national parks on either side.

## KRAKATOA

Krakatoa is an island volcano located in the Sunda Strait, south of Sumatra and west of Java in the island nation of Indonesia. Krakatoa has the distinction of causing the most violent volcanic explosion in modern times. This occurred in 1883 and was so tremendous it destroyed two-thirds of the mountain, killed 36,000 people, produced tidal waves over 120 feet high, and could be heard 3,000 miles away.

## Mount Everest

Mount Everest is the world's highest mountain and is located between Nepal and Tibet in the Himalayas. The Himalayas are a mountain range in Asia. Everest is considered to be a little over 29,000 feet high, although accurate measurement is impossible. Everest is covered with snow except for the upper level, which is kept clear by strong winds. The mountain was named after Sir George Everest, a British surveyor who led an expedition of surveyors to the mountain in 1856.

## Mount Fuji

Mount Fuji is a dormant volcano located on Honshu island, which is 70 miles southwest of Tokyo, Japan's capital. Fuji is Japan's highest mountain at 12,388 feet. There are five interconnecting lakes at the base of the mountain, providing a beautiful scene for photographers and visitors. Mount Fuji is located in Fuji-Hakone-Izu National Park and is considered sacred by Japanese Buddhists.

## Mount Kilimanjaro

Kilimanjaro is an inactive, snow-covered volcano in Africa. It has two peaks connected by a ridge. One peak is over 19,000 feet high, and the other is over 17,000 feet high. The Masai tribe live on the lower parts of the mountain. The first Europeans to discover the mountain were Germans Johannes Rebmann and Ludwig Krapf.

## Niagara Falls

Located at the north of Lake Erie on the Niagara River, Niagara Falls is not only a spectacular site for visitors, it also provides plentiful electrical energy for the area. The fast-flowing river is divided by an island into Horseshoe Falls on the Canadian side and the American Falls on the U.S. side. Horseshoe Falls is 2,600 feet long and 161 feet high, while the American Falls are 1,000 feet long and 167 feet high. There has been a great deal of erosion of the American Falls over time.

## Paricutin Volcano

Paricutin, an active volcano in Mexico, is unusual because it was formed very recently and scientists had the opportunity to see its birth. On February 20, 1943, a farmer was plowing his cornfield. He could feel the heat of the earth, and all at once an opening appeared and steam began to escape. The volcano was born. Over the next few years, the volcano erupted, completely covering one town and partially burying another. Eventually the eruptions stopped, but the town of Paricutin was buried, and San Juan Parangaricutiro was partially covered by lava and volcanic ash.

## Victoria Falls

Victoria Falls, on the border of Zambia and Zimbabwe in Africa, is more than 5,500 feet wide. The highest of the falls is almost 350 feet. The falls' African name is Mosi-oa-tunya—"the smoke that thunders," but when David Livingstone discovered the falls on November 17, 1855, he named them for Queen Victoria.

### MATTERHORN

The Matterhorn is located in the Alps mountain range on the border between Italy and Switzerland. The Matterhorn is not as tall as many other mountains. It is only 14,700 feet high, making it the third-highest peak in Europe outside of Russia. The towering snow-covered peaks make the Matterhorn one of the most difficult to climb. More climbers have died trying to scale the Matterhorn than have died on any other Alpine peak.

### SAHARA DESERT

The largest desert in the world is the Sahara Desert in northern Africa. It spans over 3,100 miles from the Atlantic Ocean to the Red Sea. It extends almost 1,400 miles from the Niger River and Lake Chad in the south to the Atlas Mountains and the Mediterranean Sea in the north. The Sahara is 3,300,000 square miles in area and covers more than 25 percent of Africa, but it is not inhabited by many people.

A desert is an area where very little rain falls. This is true in the Saraha, which is almost always dry and almost always sunny. The Sahara is also very hot, with an average annual temperature of 80 degrees F. The Sahara is not all sand as one might think of a desert. There are stony areas and mountains.

### MAUNA LOA

Located in Hawaii, Mauna Loa is the largest active volcano in the world. It rises to 13,680 feet above sea level, is 75 miles long and 65 miles wide. The crater is 591 feet deep and covers more than four square miles. Mauna Loa is one of the world's most active volcanoes. It averages an eruption about once every four years.

Name _____ Date _____

# Research on Natural Wonders of the World

Shown below are a number of questions. In order to find the answer, you need to do research in the library. First answer the question, and then list what resource you used in order to find the answer.

1. Question: Who was Angel Falls named for, and when were they discovered?

   Answer: _____

   Source: _____

2. Question: What river does Angel Falls empty into?

   Answer: _____

   Source: _____

3. Question: Who was the first European to see the Grand Canyon? In what year?

   Answer: _____

   Source: _____

4. Question: What two lakes are located at either end of the Grand Canyon?

   Answer: _____

   Source: _____

5. Question: Who discovered the Great Barrier Reef? When?

   Answer: _____

   Source: _____

6. Question: What was the name of the ship of the discoverer of the Great Barrier Reef?

   Answer: _____

   Source: _____

7. Question: What were the earliest recorded eruptions on Krakatoa?

   Answer: _____

   Source: _____

8. Question: What is the Tibetan name for Everest, and what does it mean?

   Answer: _____

   Source: _____

9. Question: Who was the first to scale Everest? When?

   Answer: _____

   Source: _____

10. Question: When was the last eruption of Mount Fuji?

    Answer: _____

    Source: _____

Name _____ Date _____

11. Question: What do the Japanese call Mount Fuji?

    Answer: _____

    Source: _____

12. Question: In what country is Mount Kilimanjaro located?

    Answer: _____

    Source: _____

13. Question: What are the names of the peaks on Kilimanjaro?

    Answer: _____

    Source: _____

14. Question: Kilimanjaro is the legendary burial spot of what famous person?

    Answer: _____

    Source: _____

15. Question: What is the name of the island that separates the Niagara River into two falls?

    Answer: _____

    Source: _____

16. Question: Who was the first European to see Niagara Falls and when?

    Answer: _____

    Source: _____

17. Question: What towns did the Paricutin volcano bury or partially bury?

    Answer: _____

    Source: _____

18. Question: Who led the first expedition to the summit of the Matterhorn? When?

    Answer: _____

    Source: _____

19. Question: What does the name "Sahara" mean?

    Answer: _____

    Source: _____

20. Question: List the nations that are located in the Sahara Desert.

    Answer: _____

    _____

    Source: _____

21. Question: What does "Mauna Loa" mean?

    Answer: _____

    Source: _____

22. Question: What is Mauna Loa's crater called?

    Answer: _____

    Source: _____

Name _____ Date _____

# Create Your Own List of the Seven Wonders of the World

You have seen the Seven Wonders of the Ancient World list that a Greek poet named Antipater assembled. These wonders were the most remarkable structures created by human beings between the years of about 3000 B.C. to A.D. 280, and all are found in a region close to Greece. Today we have an advantage over Antipater. We are aware of other magnificent structures that were built in other parts of the world during that same period as well as all of the wonderful human endeavors that have occurred since he lived.

Use your knowledge of history to create a new list of the Seven Wonders of the World. What should you consider as you create your list? Everything on the list should be something created by humans and must be remarkable because of its size, its beauty, or the engineering techniques used to make or build it. Also, take into consideration the time in which the structure was built. For example, the Great Pyramid of Giza would not be as great a challenge to build today since we have modern machines, computers, transportation, and improved building materials. The fact that it was built about 4,500 years ago with only human strength and intelligence makes it a remarkable accomplishment.

Listed below are some of the structures you may want to include in your list, or you may add something not listed. After you have created your list, write a short essay explaining why you included the items you did and possibly why you omitted other items you may think others will put into their lists. Use your own paper.

- The Great Pyramid of Giza
- The Statue of Zeus at Olympia
- The Mausoleum at Halicarnassus
- The Lighthouse of Alexandria
- The Catacombs of Alexandria
- The Leaning Tower of Pisa
- The Mosque of Hagia Sophia
- The Washington Monument
- Taj Mahal in Agra, India
- Motherland statue in Volgograd, Russia
- The Statue of Liberty in New York City
- The Aztec Temple in Mexico
- The Incan city of Machu Picchu, Peru
- The Statues on Easter Island
- The Parthenon in Athens, Greece
- Stonehenge in England
- The Channel Tunnel ("Chunnel")
- The Golden Gate Bridge in San Francisco
- Hoover Dam in Arizona/Nevada, USA
- The Statue of Corcovado Christ in Rio de Janeiro
- The Hanging Gardens of Babylon
- The Temple of Artemis at Ephesus
- The Colossus of Rhodes
- The Colosseum of Rome
- The Great Wall of China
- The Porcelain Tower of Nanking
- The Sydney Opera House in Australia
- The Eiffel Tower in Paris, France
- The Empire State Building, New York City
- Mount Rushmore in South Dakota, USA
- Angkor Wat in Cambodia
- The Panama Canal
- The Mayan Temples of Guatemala
- The Palace of Persepolis in Iran
- Petra, the rock-carved city in Jordan
- The Temple of the Inscriptions in Mexico
- Big Ben in London, England
- The High Dam in Aswan, Egypt
- Itaipú Dam in Brazil/Paraguay
- The Suez Canal in Egypt

# Answer Keys

### List and Locate the Seven Wonders of the World (page 2)

| Wonder | Location | Date | Builder or Designer | Purpose |
|---|---|---|---|---|
| 1. The Great Pyramid of Giza | Egypt | 2580 B.C. | Egyptian Kings | Tomb |
| 2. The Hanging Gardens of Babylon | Babylon | 600 B.C. | Nebuchadnezzar | For wife's pleasure |
| 3. The Statue of Zeus at Olympia | Olympia | 560 B.C. | Phidias | Honor Zeus |
| 4. The Temple of Artemis at Ephesus | Ephesus | 450 B.C. | Croesus | Honor Artemis |
| 5. The Mausoleum at Halicarnassus | Halicarnassus | 353 B.C. | Mausolus | Tomb |
| 6. The Colossus of Rhodes | Rhodes | 290 B.C. | Chares | To Honor Helios |
| 7. The Lighthouse of Alexandria | Alexandria | 280 B.C. | Sostratos or Alexander | For sailors |

### The Seven Wonders of the Ancient World: What did they look like? (page 3)

1. G
2. F
3. D
4. E
5. B
6. A
7. C

### The Seven Wonders of the Ancient World: Where Would They Be Today? (page 4)

| Name of Wonder | Country Located Today |
|---|---|
| 1. The Lighthouse of Alexandria | Egypt |
| 2. The Hanging Gardens of Babylon | Iraq |
| 3. The Temple of Artemis at Ephesus | Turkey |
| 4. The Great Pyramid of Giza | Egypt |
| 5. The Mausoleum at Halicarnassus | Turkey |
| 6. The Colossus of Rhodes | Off the coast of Turkey |
| 7. The Statue of Zeus at Olympia | Greece |

### The Great Pyramid Quiz (page 7)

1. limestone
2. True
3. ramp
4. True
5. pharaoh
6. million
7. Khufu or Cheops
8. Cairo
9. True
10. True
11. three
12. Nile
13. sledge
14. burial chamber
15. higher
16. tons
17. True
18. logs
19. 0.1
20. True

9. pharaoh
10. weepers
11. papyrus
12. cartonnage
13. sledge
14. bier
15. pyramid
16. catacombs
17. hieroglyphics

### Ancient Egyptian Terms (page 10)

1. Book of the Dead
2. amulet
3. scribe
4. mummy case
5. Overseer of Mysteries
6. mummification
7. Osiris
8. Field of Reeds

### Three World Conquerors Who Invaded Egypt (page 11)

1. N
2. A
3. C
4. N
5. N
6. A
7. C
8. A
9. C
10. N
11. C
12. N
13. C
14. A
15. C
16. N
17. N
18. N
19. A
20. A
21. A
22. N
23. C

**The Hanging Gardens of Babylon Quiz (page 15)**
1. superior
2. True
3. on the roof
4. True
5. Gate of the Gods
6. an interior court
7. True
8. animals
9. invaders
10. True
11. True
12. True
13. True
14. True
15. Persia
16. Euphrates
17. True
18. fountains
19. Hanging Gardens
20. Roman

**Hanging Gardens of Babylon Crossword Puzzle (page 19)**

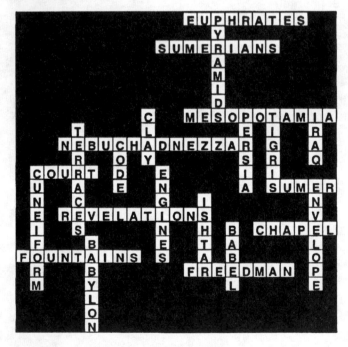

**Hammurabi's Code (pages 20–22)**
Answers will vary

**The Statue of Zeus Quiz (page 24)**
1. an earthquake
2. Zeus
3. religious
4. True
5. True
6. Phidias
7. True
8. Nike
9. True
10. fire
11. True
12. Olympic Games
13. True
14. True
15. True
16. wood
17. ivory
18. gold
19. gems
20. True

**Greek Temples in Your Town (page 25)**
Answers will vary, but might include.
1. Lincoln Memorial
2. U.S. Capitol
3. White House
4. Supreme Court Building
5. Many buildings in Washington, D.C.
6. Many banks
7. Many museums

**Research on Temples (page 26)**
1. **Corinthian:** A type of Greek architecture that is elegant and elaborately ornate. The top of a Corinthian column features acanthus leaves.
2. **Doric:** A form of Greek architecture known for its simplicity and austerity. The top of a Doric column is plain.
3. **Ionic:** A type of architecture known for grace and elegance. The top of an Ionic column has the appearance of ram's horns.
4. **Frieze:** A decorative border, around the upper part of a wall.
5. **Parthenon:** A temple honoring Athena that was built on the Acropolis.
6. **Facade:** A veneer or artificial front.
7. **Capital:** The top part of a pillar or column.

**Olympic Games Synonyms (page 29)**
1. A
2. B
3. B
4. A
5. C
6. A
7. A
8. C
9. B
10. A
11. C
12. A
13. C
14. A
15. B

## The Temple of Artemis at Ephesus Quiz (page 33)
1. True
2. True
3. animals
4. True
5. Croesus
6. marble
7. True
8. True
9. St. Paul
10. True
11. Leto
12. True
13. marble
14. True
15. larger
16. True
17. Alexander the Great
18. True
19. True
20. Ephesus

## Research On Greek Life (page 34)
1. **Acropolis**: A hill in ancient Athens. It eventually became a religious center.
2. **agora**: The market-place and civic center of a Greek town where people gathered to visit.
3. **ostracism**: A method of controlling politicians who were becoming too influential. They were banished for 10 years
4. **demi-gods**: Mythical creatures who were thought to be part human and part god.
5. **epic poetry**: A long poem that tells the story of historical events or heroes.
6. **oracle**: A priest or priestess who could reveal the thoughts of the gods, give advice, and forecast the future. It was also a place where the gods and goddesses spoke.
7. **polis**: A city-state.

## Temple of Artemis Word Search (page 35)

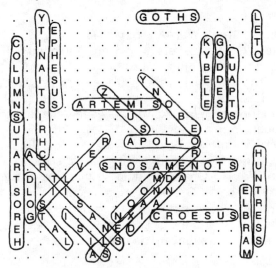

## Greek and Roman Gods (page 36)

| Greek God | Roman God |
|---|---|
| 1. Poseidon | Neptune |
| 2. Eros | Cupid |
| 3. Ares | Mars |
| 4. Hestia | Vesta |
| 5. Artemis | Diana |
| 6. Athena | Minerva |
| 7. Demeter | Ceres |
| 8. Hades | Pluto |
| 9. Aphrodite | Venus |
| 10. Hephaistos | Vulcan |
| 11. Hera | Juno |
| 12. Zeus | Jupiter |
| 13. Herakles | Hercules |
| 14. Persephone | Proserpina |
| 15. Hermes | Mercury |
| 16. Hypnos | Somnus |
| 17. Kronos | Saturn |
| 18. Odysseus | Ulysses |
| 19. Pan | Faunus |
| 20. Dionysus | Bacchus |

## Greek Gods and Goddesses From A to Z (page 37)
1. Gorgon
2. Apollo
3. Erida
4. Eros
5. Pan
6. Erinyes
7. Dione
8. Graces
9. Helios
10. Hades
11. Medusa
12. Hebe
13. Poseidon
14. Artemis
15. Hera
16. Hephaistos
17. Fates
18. Ares
19. Hypnos
20. Hermes
21. Herakles
22. Hestia
23. Kronos
24. Zeus

25. Gods And Goddesses From A To Z

## The Mausoleum at Halicarnassus Quiz (page 40)
1. Greek
2. king
3. True
4. True
5. sister
6. Persia
7. True
8. True
9. son
10. Ephesus
11. beauty
12. True
13. True
14. burial
15. goddesses or warriors
16. True
17. True
18. centuries
19. True
20. used for other building projects

## Burial and Death Terms (page 42)
1. catacombs
2. crematorium
3. hearse
4. bier
5. monument
6. mummification
7. mausoleum
8. cenotaph
9. sarcophagus
10. wake
11. crypt
12. mortuary
13. shroud
14. corpse
15. burial ground
16. coffin
17. cemetery
18. epitaph
19. eulogy
20. embalm
21. mortician
22. mourner

## It's Greek To Me Crossword Puzzle (page 43)

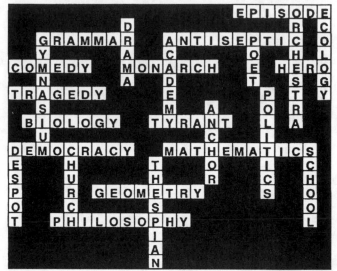

## The Colossus of Rhodes Quiz (page 46)
1. True
2. Mediterranean
3. True
4. True
5. True
6. Sun
7. True
8. 12
9. True
10. True
11. True
12. Iron
13. Bronze
14. True
15. earthquake
16. Stones
17. oracle
18. True
19. True
20. Syria

## Research on Greek Warfare (page 47)
1. **hoplites**: Greek soldiers who were equipped with armor, shield, spear, and a sword.
2. **hopla**: The weapons of the hoplites—spear, sword, shield, and helmet.
3. **Peloponnesian War**: A war between Athens and Sparta fought from 431 to 404 B.C.
4. **Battle of Marathon**: Fought in 490 B.C., the Greeks were able to repel an invasion during the Persian Wars.
5. **Trojan War**: In Greek mythology, this was a war between a number of Greek city-states against Troy.
6. **phalanx**: A fighting maneuver used by the hoplites. They formed several lines, locked their shields together, and held their spears forward as they advanced.

**The Lighthouse at Alexandria Quiz (page 50)**
1. True
2. soldiers and workers
3. a ramp
4. True
5. a Greek god
6. True
7. True
8. Pharos
9. pharos
10. an earthquake
11. True
12. Alexander the Great
13. True
14. True
15. brass
16. True
17. True
18. rectangular
19. True
20. cylinder

**Sailing and Trading in Greece (page 52)**
1. rudder
2. aft
3. fore
4. ferry
5. wharf
6. breakwater
7. cargo
8. galley
9. smuggler
10. longshoreman
11. porter
12. money-changers
13. boatswain
14. skipper
15. seaworthy
16. freighter
17. barter
18. 'round ship'
19. prow
20. battering ram

**Archaeology Quiz (page 54)**
1. museum
2. excavating
3. A.D.
4. carbon dating
5. expedition
6. B.C.
7. trial trenches
8. relic
9. trial shafts
10. trowel
11. archaeologist
12. archaeology
13. artifact
14. site
15. ancient
16. catalog
17. civilization
18. culture
19. translate
20. manuscripts

**Stonehenge Vocabulary (page 56)**
1. barge
2. monument
3. megalith
4. quarry
5. Stonehenge
6. bluestones
7. sledge
8. lintel
9. astronomy
10. prehistoric
11. Neolithic
12. astronomical observatory
13. axis
14. sarsen
15. Druids
16. trilithons
17. henge

**Great Wall of China Synonyms (page 58)**
1. A
2. B
3. C
4. B
5. B
6. A
7. C
8. A
9. A
10. B
11. C
12. A
13. B
14. C
15. A

**Colosseum Vocabulary (page 60)**
1. tier
2. Doric
3. amphitheater
4. Colosseum
5. Corinthian
6. substructure
7. Ionic
8. arcade
9. pilaster

10. corridor
11. arch
12. ramp
13. aristocracy
14. forum
15. gallery
16. elliptical
17. sea battles
18. Vespasian
19. common people
20. emperor

## Terms in Ancient Roman Life Crossword (page 64)

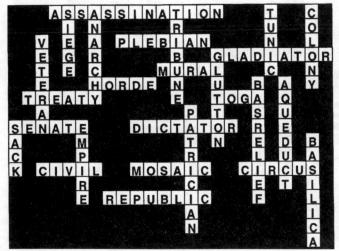

## Taj Mahal Vocabulary (pages 66–67)

1. A
2. D
3. B
4. C
5. D
6. D
7. A
8. C
9. B
10. D
11. B
12. D
13. A
14. B
15. A
16. C
17. A
18. B
19. D
20. D
21. C
22. B

## Comparing The Statue of Liberty With The Colossus of Rhodes (page 70)

1. On Liberty Island (Bedloe's Island) in New York Harbor, New York City, U.S.A.
2. Originally called *Liberty Enlightening the World.*, the statue's left arm is a tablet with the date of the Declaration of Independence written in Roman numerals, her right arm is held high and has a torch lighting the way and welcoming immigrants and visitors. At the statue's feet is a broken chain, which symbolizes how the United States broke free from Great Britain.
3. Frédéric Auguste Bartholdi
4. A gift from France to celebrate their friendship and freedom.
5. A steel framework covered with copper sheeting.
6. Initial Cost to Build the Statue: $400,000: Initial Cost of Pedestal: $270,000
7. Height of Pedestal: 89 ft.
8. Height: Base to torch: 151 ft.; Foundation to torch: 305 ft.; Head to foot: 111 ft.
9. Erected and unveiled on October 26,1886.
10. Weight of copper: 100 tons; Weight of steel: 125 tons; Total weight: 225 tons

## Research on Statues (pages 73–74)

1. Limestone.
2. A manifestation of their sun god
3. Khufu or Cheops
4. He became king
5. Admiral Roggeveen in 1722.
6. Dutch
7. He discovered the Island on Easter Day.
8. Chile.
9. Gutzon Borglum, the sculpture.
10. A marble bust of Abraham Lincoln that sits in the U.S. Capitol, a bronze statue of Philip Sheridan, figures on the Cathedral of Saint John in New York City, and he worked on the large sculpture of the leaders of the Confederacy on Stone Mountain Georgia.
11. Washington
12. Jefferson
13. Silicosis
14. Paul Landowski
15. It took five years to compete and was finished in 1931.

## Identifying Well-Known Statues (page 75)

| Name | Location |
| --- | --- |
| 1. Corcovado Christ | Rio de Janeiro, Brazil |
| 2. Great Sphinx | Giza, Egypt |
| 3. Statue of Liberty | New York City, U.S.A |
| 4. Abraham Lincoln | Washington D.C., U.S.A. |
| 5. Mount Rushmore Sculptures | South Dakota, U.S.A. |
| 6. Iwo Jima Memorial | Arlington, VA., U.S.A. |
| 7. Stone Mountain | Atlanta, GA, U.S.A. |
| 8. Easter Island Statues | Easter Island (Chile) Pacific Ocean |

**Buildings, Temples, and Monuments (pages 76–77)**

| Name | Location |
| --- | --- |
| 1. Eiffel Tower | Paris, France |
| 2. Great Wall of China | China |
| 3. Colosseum | Rome, Italy |
| 4. Stonehenge | Salisbury, England |
| 5. Gateway Arch | St. Louis, MO, U.S.A. |
| 6. Pyramid | Giza, Egypt |
| 7. Sydney Opera House | Sydney, Australia |
| 8. Space Needle | Seattle, Washington, U.S.A. |
| 9. Washington Monument | Washington, D.C., U.S.A. |
| 10. Big Ben | London, England |
| 11. Golden Gate Bridge | San Francisco, CA, U.S.A. |
| 12. Taj Mahal | Agra, India |
| 13. Leaning Tower of Pisa | Pisa, Italy |
| 14. Parthenon | Athens, Greece |
| 15. St. Basil's Cathedral | Moscow, Russia |
| 16. Arc de Triomphe | Paris, France |
| 17. Lincoln Memorial | Washington, D.C., U.S.A. |
| 18. St. Paul's Cathedral | London, England |

**Research on Natural Wonders of the World (pages 82–83)**

1. James Angel, a U.S. explorer and aviator, discovered the falls in 1935.
2. The Caroni River, which is a tributary of the Orinoco River
3. Garcia Lopez de Cardenas, a Spanish explorer, in 1540
4. Lake Mead and Lake Powell
5. The reef was discovered by Capt. James Cook on June 11, 1770.
6. *Endeavor*
7. 1680–81
8. Chomolungma. It means "goddess mother of the world."
9. Edmund Hillary and his party reached the top on May 29,1953.
10. 1707
11. Fujiyama
12. It is in Tanzania close to the border with Kenya.
13. Kibo and Mawenzi
14. King Solomon
15. Goat Island
16. Father Louis Hennep in 1678
17. Paricutin was buried, and San Juan Parangaricutiro was partially buried.
18. Edward Whymper, a British explorer, on July 14, 1865
19. Sahara is taken from the Arabic word for "desert" or "steppe."
20. Morocco, Tunisia, Mali, Niger, Chad, and Sudan have large desert regions, and most of Western Sahara, Algeria, Libya, Egypt, and Mauritania are located in the Sahara.
21. Long mountain
22. Mokuaweoweo

# Internet Resources

If you would like to research some of the topics explored in this book, the Internet has many sites that provide excellent starting points. Start by using the subjects or keywords below to find sites that contain useful information.

Seven Wonders of the Ancient World

Great Pyramid of Giza

Hanging Gardens of Babylon

Statue of Zeus of Olympia

Temple of Artemis at Ephesus

Mausoleum at Halicarnassus

Colossus of Rhodes

Lighthouse of Alexandria

Egypt

Mummies

Tombs

Nebuchadnezzar

Mesopotamia

Greek Mythology

Pharos

Stonehenge

Great Wall of China

Colosseum

Taj Mahal

Statue of Liberty

Great Sphinx

Easter Island

Mount Rushmore

Corcovado Christ

Iwo Jima Memorial

Stone Mountain

Eiffel Tower

St. Louis Gateway Arch

Sydney Opera House

Seattle Space Needle

Washington Monument

Big Ben

Golden Gate Bridge

Leaning Tower of Pisa

Parthenon

St. Basil's Cathedral

Arc de Triomphe

Lincoln Memorial

St. Paul's Cathedral

Mosque of Hagia Sophia

Angkor Wat in Cambodia

Machu Picchu, Peru

Petra, Jordan

Hoover Dam

Porcelain Tower of Nanking

Aztec Temple in Mexico

Mayan Temple in Guatemala

Palace of Persepolis in Iran

Temple of the Inscriptions in Mexico

High Dam in Aswan, Egypt

Itaipú Dam in Brazil/Paraguay

Natural Wonders of the World

Angel Falls

Grand Canyon

Great Barrier Reef

Iguacu Falls

Krakatoa

Mount Everest

Mount Fuji

Mount Kilimanjaro

Niagara Falls

Paricutin Volcano

Victoria Falls

Matterhorn

Sahara Desert

Mauna Loa